Educational institutions and their environments: managing the boundaries

OPEN UNIVERSITY PRESS

Management in Education Series

Editor

Tony Bush

Senior Lecturer in Educational Policy and Management
at The Open University

The series comprises five volumes which cover important topics within the field of educational management. The articles present examples of theory and practice in school and college management. The authors discuss many of the major issues of relevance to educational managers in the post-Education Reform Act era.

The five readers are components of The Open University M.A. in Education module *E818 Management in Education*. Further information about this course and the M.A. programme may be obtained by writing to the Higher Degrees Office, The Open University, PO Box 49, Walton Hall, Milton Keynes, MK7 6AD.

TITLES IN THE SERIES

Managing Education: Theory and Practice
Tony Bush (ed.)

Approaches to Curriculum Management
Margaret Preedy (ed.)

Financial Management in Education
Rosalind Levačić (ed.)

Human Resource Management in Education
Colin Riches and Colin Morgan (eds)

Educational Institutions and their Environments:
Managing the Boundaries
Ron Glatter (ed.)

Educational institutions and their environments: managing the boundaries

EDITED BY

Ron Glatter

at The Open University

OPEN UNIVERSITY PRESS
MILTON KEYNES · PHILADELPHIA
in association with The Open University

Open University Press
12 Cofferidge Close
Stony Stratford
Milton Keynes MK11 1BY

and
1900 Frost Road, Suite 101
Bristol, PA 19007, USA

First Published 1989

British Library Cataloguing in Publication Data
Educational institutions and their environments:
    managing the boundaries.—(Management in education)
    1. Great Britain. Educational institutions.
    Management
    I. Glatter, Ron   II. Series
    371.2′00941

    ISBN 0-335-09245-4
        0-335-09244-6 (paper)

Library of Congress Cataloging in Publication Number Available

Typeset by Rowland Phototypesetting Ltd
Bury St Edmunds, Suffolk
Printed in Great Britain by Biddles Ltd
Guildford and King's Lynn

Contents

Acknowledgements

All possible care has been taken to trace ownership of the material included in this volume, and Open University Press would like to make grateful acknowledgement for permission to reproduce it here.

1   P. Scott (1989). Commissioned for this collection.
2   L. G. Bolman and T. E. Deal (1984). *Modern Approaches to Understanding and Managing Organizations*, pp. 42–9, San Francisco, Jossey-Bass Inc.
3   W. K. Hoy and C. G. Miskel (1987). *Educational Administration: Theory, Research and Practice*, pp. 86–107, New York, McGraw-Hill Book Company, Inc.
4   L. Gray (1989). Commissioned for this collection.
5   A. Westoby (1989). Commissioned for this collection.
6   C. Pascal (1987). 'Democratised primary school government conflicts and dichotomies', *Educational Management and Administration*, Vol. 15, No. 3, pp. 193–202, Longman Group Limited.
7   G. Mitchell (1987). 'Community education and school: a commentary', *Community Education* edited by Allen *et al.*, pp. 87–99, Milton Keynes, Open University Press.
8   D. Parkes and C. Thomson (1989). Commissioned for this collection.
9   J. Mann (1989). Commissioned for this collection.

I should like to thank Jane Goodey for her efficient and painstaking work in connection with preparing the manuscript for publication, and Helen Knowles for her careful typing and secretarial work in bringing the contributions together. Responsibility for any remaining errors or omissions rests with the editor alone.

The following contributors are those whose work was specially prepared for this volume:

Ron Glatter   Director of the Centre for Educational Policy and Management, The Open University School of Education.

Lynton Gray   Head of the Educational Management Service, North East London Polytechnic.

John Mann   An educational consultant and writer and formerly Director of Education for the London Borough of Harrow.

David Parkes   On attachment to the European Institute of Education and Social Policy in Paris and was Director of the Responsive College Programme at the Further Education Staff College.

Peter Scott   Editor of *The Times Higher Education Supplement*.

Craig Thomson   Marketing Manager of Stroud College, Gloucestershire, and was Co-ordinator of the Responsive College Programme at the Further Education Staff College.

Adam Westoby   Senior Lecturer in Education, The Open University School of Education.

Introduction: Coping with a new climate

Ron Glatter

The focus of this book

This book is about educational institutions' relations with their 'environments'. It consists of a set of articles, some reprinted and some specially prepared for this volume, dealing with organization–environment relationships and various approaches to the management of these. A number of the articles take a general view, examining some of the key concepts which are relevant to this topic, whereas others focus on specific types of linkage, for example between schools and parents or between colleges and their 'clients'.

It is intended through this volume to place 'external management' more firmly on the agenda both of managers in educational institutions and of students of educational management. The book may encourage reflection about what knowledge, skills and attitudes are needed for managing the environment effectively and what directions might most usefully be followed in developing theory, research and practice in this area.

Recent legislation relating to schools, colleges and institutions of higher education has stimulated two movements which have great significance for the nature of management in education. First, the relative autonomy of institutions has been enhanced. They have been given greater control over their own affairs and more scope for self-government and 'local' management. Secondly, the opportunity for users of educational services such as parents, students and employers to choose between institutions (and also, in some cases, to exercise influence within them) has been extended. This has created a climate of heightened inter–institutional competition and a sense of greater dependence on external audiences. Both developments imply a more explicit, visible and broad-ranging managerial role for many staff in education and a need for them to acquire new skills and competences to enable them to carry it out effectively.

These developments have accentuated a trend that has been apparent at least since the mid-1960s – when the Plowden Committee (1967) demonstrated the significance of the connection between home and school for children's learning at primary school level – towards a sharper focus on schools' and colleges' interactions with their environments. The nature of these interactions has seemed increasingly important both for the effectiveness of their educational provision and for their survival and growth as institutions. However, although this area has been the subject of much public and professional debate, the literature and research relating to external management in education is still very sparse. (It should be added that at the time of writing there were signs of growing activity.)

If the external management role of staff in education has grown in importance, how well equipped are they to carry it out? As with financial management, the point is often made that they have not generally been prepared by experience or training to tackle it. Writing of secondary school heads, Morgan *et al.* (1983, p. 16) argued that 'In the public domain, the head . . . has a responsibility for external communication, dialogue, report and accountability which, in terms of previous professional career, is likely to be a largely new experience.' Surveys of secondary school heads have, however, found that they do not generally consider their external duties to present serious difficulties (Jones, 1987; Weindling and Earley, 1987). This may, as Jones suggests, result from a general underestimation of the significance of these responsibilities. Although in her survey aspects of the external relations role were rated by heads as low priorities for training (and were apparently not enjoyed by the heads), their responses raised questions about their approach to this area. Apparently, the only members of the community they mentioned were the parents, while governors and the local education authority (LEA) were:

> mentioned almost totally in negative terms, as interfering and/or amateur nuisances who detract from the Head's autonomy. . . . Heads seem to see their needs in terms of internal survival skills rather than in terms of their important role as mediator of the external relations of the school.
>
> (Jones, 1987, pp. 60–61)

This survey of 400 secondary heads was conducted in the early 1980s. It may be that, as a result of the legislative changes since then, attitudes to the 'external domain' of professional leadership (Hughes, 1985) have been changing. At the time of writing, a growth in private consultancy services offering to help institutions with their external relations seemed likely and 'guide books' had begun to appear (e.g. Keen and Greenall, 1987).

'Institution' and 'environment': An artificial distinction

The concept of an institution's 'environment' which is central to this book is an admittedly arbitrary one and even potentially misleading. As Starbuck

(1976, p. 1069) has noted: 'Assuming organizations can be sharply distinguished from their environments distorts reality by compressing into one
dichotomy a melange of continuously varying phenomena.' The distinction
is essentially artificial and pragmatic, and although it can be useful analyti-
cally, its arbitrariness should be continually borne in mind when reading the
chapters that follow.

For example, in education it is particularly difficult to determine
whether certain groups of 'stakeholders', such as pupils/students, parents and
governors, should be regarded as internal or external to the institution.
Where do the boundaries actually fall, and how permeable are they? Governors are an obvious case in point, especially following the recent legislation.
They are now to have a wide-ranging set of decision-making responsibilities
in major areas of a school's or college's activities such as finance, staffing and
the curriculum. On this basis, they might well be 'placed' within rather than
outside the institution, especially if the analogy (heard with increasing
frequency) with the board of directors of a company is regarded as valid. But
an important part of the justification for reforming the composition of
governing bodies has been to give the 'consumer' a greater and more direct
influence in institutional decision making. Hence the substantial increase in
parental and community representation on school governing bodies, and in
the representation of employment interests on the governing bodies of
colleges of further education. Hence also the growing interest of 'consumer'
organizations such as the National Consumer Council and the Advisory
Centre for Education in the work of school governors. Indeed, one of the
major unanswered questions for the 1990s is whether governing bodies will
become identified with, and perhaps provide a source of additional strength
to, the existing 'internal' management structure at the expense of 'external'
interests, or whether the latter will be able to exert some significant influence
upon the policies to be pursued by internal 'office-holders', possibly on the
(ideal) model of the relationship between a democratic legislature and its
executive.

Pupils and students offer another example of this dilemma of allocation.
At least for analytical purposes, from a management perspective, they would
generally be regarded as members of the institution. Yet (with the possible
exception of higher education) they reflect the local environment in ways that
are often of crucial importance for both institutional management and
teaching. As Bollen and Robin (1985, p. 90) have observed, in writing about
the context for school improvement, 'The context is *outside* the system by
definition, but works *in* the system. . . . Noticing pupil behaviour in the
classroom brings us to the social–economic aspects of the neighbourhood.'

The particular allocation made in each case may reflect a value position,
a personal view about the desirable relationship of that particular group of
stakeholders with the institution. For example, someone with a strong
orientation towards community education is likely to define the 'boundaries'
between an educational institution and its environment rather differently

from someone who sees the institution's prime task in terms of satisfying market demands. For the community educator, the boundaries would be inclusive and permeable. For the 'marketeer' they would be exclusive and fairly firm. However, these two individuals, if they were institutional managers, would both exhibit an emphasis on external management and some of their actual policies and practices might not therefore differ as sharply as their ideological differences would imply. They might both, for instance, give attention to discovering 'customer' preferences and searching for opportunities for 'diversification'. Someone who sees the institution as existing mainly to provide high-quality professional educational services to a relatively assured clientele would also be inclined to draw fairly tight boundaries and, in addition, to give most emphasis to internal management, for example professional leadership of staff and curriculum evaluation.

Allocating a particular group to one category rather than the other may simply reflect a specific situation. For example, Kogan *et al.* (1984, p. 52) imply that regarding a school governing body as conceptually 'separate' from 'their' school would be more accurate in some instances than in others. What accounts for these differences? Numerous factors will be involved, including variations in local context, ethos and personalities. The following chapters throw some light on these issues, and it is hoped they will stimulate reflection and a search for more effective ways of managing the relations between institutions and their environments.

Outline of the book

The book is divided into two sections. Section I consists of four chapters in which some of the central concepts which are relevant to relations between educational institutions and their environments are examined.

In Chapter 1, Scott examines the key concepts of accountability, responsiveness and responsibility against the background of the current policy context in education. He regards the idea of responsiveness in particular as complex and subtle, and warns of the danger 'that a simple-minded, one-dimensional, tough-talking definition of responsiveness in education will be adopted'. If responsiveness is a many-sided notion, then managing relations between institutions and their environments should also be a complex and multifaceted activity, and in selecting the remaining contributions an attempt has been made to reflect such a broad approach to our theme.

Bolman and Deal present a brief commentary on research into the relationships between the structure, technology (in a wide sense) and environment of organizations in Chapter 2. They develop a contingency approach, and stress the need for 'complex, differentiated and flexible' structures for organizations to cope effectively with turbulent and uncertain environments.

In Chapter 3, Hoy and Miskel provide a much longer and denser review of theory and research on organizations and their environments, with particular reference to schools, looking at relevant models and their implications for organizational design and management practice.

The final chapter in Section I presents a discussion by Gray of marketing and some of its applications to schools and colleges. Parallels are drawn with other service industries, but the need for marketing principles and practices to be adapted to fit the purposes of educational institutions is also stressed.

In Section II we move away from a focus on overarching concepts to examine a selected range of relationships. The intention has not been to present a comprehensive coverage. There are so many different types of connections that such an approach is scarcely practicable and its results would probably not in any case be very enlightening. The emphasis here is on a few linkages which seem to have particular significance in the contemporary policy and management context.

In Chapter 5, Westoby considers relationships between school and parents in the wake of the 1986 and 1988 Education Acts. He looks both at the impact on this relationship of wider parental choice and a more competitive climate, drawing on relevant theory and research, and also at the prospects for greater parental influence upon decision making within schools.

Chapter 6 offers an analysis by Pascal of some of the major dilemmas concerning the operation of school governing bodies. Although the article is based on research conducted prior to the legislation of the late 1980s, the issues raised, of élitism versus pluralism, centralization versus devolution, professionals versus laity and support versus accountability, are likely to remain central ones in the 1990s: if anything, they will probably become sharper.

Some of the thrusts of the new legislation, particularly the focus on parental choice and the orientation towards consumerism, appear antithetical to some of the more ambitious community education experiments of the past few decades. However, the measures might be seen as providing incentives for staff to be more outward-looking and to build more external connections to help their institutions to survive in the marketplace. In Chapter 7, Mitchell examines the potential for, and problems of, developing community education practice from the institutional base of the school, not only for designated 'community schools' but also for others that seek to develop a community 'dimension' to their work.

The broad question of how to develop effective links between an educational institution and its 'clientele' was addressed in the context of further education by the large-scale Responsive College Programme (RCP), funded by the Manpower Services Commission (now the Training Agency). In Chapter 8, Parkes and Thomson summarize the approach which underlay this venture and offer some conclusions about how to 'manage the gaps' between colleges and clients. They also present a case study from the Programme which focuses on one of the RCP's major areas of concern, that of 'customer communication', an area which is likely to be of interest well beyond FE. This chapter should be considered in conjunction with Scott's discussion of responsiveness (Chapter 1) and Gray's review of marketing in education (Chapter 4).

The growth in institutional autonomy is occurring at the same time as the role and responsibilities of LEAs are undergoing very significant change. Those schools (assumed to be the majority) that remain within the LEA system and almost all colleges will need to develop radically changed relationships with their authorities. In Chapter 9, Mann considers how LEAs' new tasks are likely to impact upon the institutions and ways in which the latter might manage the relationship in order to maximize its value to them.

Clearly there are other key relationships which might have been included, for example with other educational institutions (Open University, 1988) or with the network of external support for pupil welfare (Johnson *et al.*, 1980). In such areas, it was not possible either to identify suitable recently published material or to arrange for original contributions to be prepared. It is hoped, however, that the chapters in Section II offer a sufficient representation of key relationships to stimulate further work focusing on the interface between institutions and their environments.

Finally, it will be clear by now that the major concern of this volume is not with the institution's total environment but only with that part of it over which some influence can be exerted. Thus the broad social, economic and policy context within which institutions operate are, with the partial exception of Chapter 1, treated lightly if at all in these contributions. This book is intended for those with management responsibilities in education. Certainly these people need to understand and respond to such broader forces, but management, like politics, is the art of the possible, its concern is with action – preferably informed by reflection (Schon, 1984). So the emphasis in these pages is on the institution's immediate or local environment. Even then, questions arise about what factors are amenable to influence from the institution. Bollen and Robin (1985, p. 96) suggest some key questions for educational managers considering their context in relation to plans for institutional development:

> What does it mean to us that the context looks like this? And, is there a strategy to deal with a context of this sort? Which factors can we do something about, and to which must we adapt?

References

Bollen, R. and Robin, D. (1985). School improvement context. In Van Velzen, W. *et al. (eds), Making School Improvement Work: A Conceptual Guide to Practice.* OECD/CERI International School Improvement Project, Leuven (Belgium) Acco.

Hughes, M. (1985). Leadership in professionally-staffed organizations. In Hughes, M., Ribbins, P. and Thomas, H. (eds), *Managing Education: The System and Institution*. London, Holt, Rhinehart and Winston.

Johnson, D., Ransom, E., Packwood, T., Bowden, K. and Kogan, M. (1980). *Secondary Schools and the Welfare Network*. London, George Allen and Unwin.

Jones, A. (1987). *Leadership for Tomorrow's Schools*. Oxford, Basil Blackwell.

Keen, C. and Greenall, J. (1987). *Public Relations Management in Colleges, Polytechnics and Universities*. Banbury, HEIST.

Kogan, M., Johnson, D., Packwood, P. and Whitaker, T. (1984). *School Governing Bodies*. London, Heinemann.

Morgan, C., Hall, V. and Mackay, H. (1983). *The Selection of Secondary School Headteachers*. Milton Keynes, Open University Press.

Open University (1988). Other schools and colleges. Part 6 of Block 6 'The School's External Relations', Open University course E325 *Managing Schools*. Milton Keynes, Open University Press.

Plowden Committee (1967). *Children and their Primary Schools*. Central Advisory Council for Education. London, HMSO.

Schon, D. A. (1984). Leadership as reflection-in-action. In Sergiovanni, T. and Corbally, J. (eds), *Leadership and Organizational Culture*. Urbana, University of Illinois Press.

Starbuck, W. H. (1976). Organizations and their environments. In Dunnette, M. D. (ed.), *Handbook of Industrial and Organizational Psychology*. Chicago, Rand McNally.

Weindling, D. and Earley, P. (1987). *Secondary Headship: the First Years*. Windsor, NFER-Nelson.

Section I

Key concepts

1

Accountability, responsiveness and responsibility

Peter Scott

The changing context of educational policy

For more than 10 years there has been increasing emphasis on the need for schools, colleges, polytechnics and universities to be more responsive to students and employers, more accountable to taxpayers (and to government which acts as their proxy), and more responsible for their own efficiency and effectiveness. These trends are commonly associated with the resurgence of more traditional notions about the content, style and organization of education. This resurgence first broke through the crust of politics in 1976 when the Prime Minister, James Callaghan, in a speech at Ruskin College, Oxford, questioned many of the progressive assumptions made by education during the 1960s. It gathered force when a Conservative Government was elected in 1979. In a modified form these conservative notions have been enshrined in the Education Reform Act of 1988, a coherent legislative attempt to modify the post-war consensus which had grown out of the 1944 Education Act. It can therefore be argued that the emphasis on accountability, responsiveness and responsibility was part of this wide movement to reimpose conservative values and practices in education, if only in the weak sense that the existing system, from the primary school to the university, was regarded by its critics as unaccountable, unresponsive and irresponsible.

However, to see accountability, responsiveness and responsibility simply and exclusively as the goals of traditionalists determined to subvert a progressive post-war consensus, is misleading. It can well be argued that these qualities have always been emphasized within schools and colleges; certainly further education was, and is, organized around the principle of responsiveness to both students and employers, while the comprehensive reorganization of secondary schools in the 1960s can plausibly be attributed to customer dissatisfaction with the old division into grammar and secondary modern schools. It can also be argued that the accountability of education to the representatives of the communities which it serves has not been enhanced by the erosion of the responsibilities of local authorities, whether for expenditure level or for educational management. Nor is it clear that the increasing subordination of the universities to the direction first of the University Grants Committee (UGC) and now the Universities Funding Council (UFC) has encouraged the responsible self-management of those institutions. So it is by no means a settled question that reforms in the organization of education since 1976 – or 1979 – have made schools and colleges more responsive, accountable and responsible.

Another reason for not aligning the increasing emphasis on these three qualities with the recent drive to reform the system is that, both in principle and in practice, they often come into conflict. For example, there is a tension between the desire to make education more accountable, generally in order to encourage the more appropriate and efficient use of resources, and the wish to make institutions more responsible for their future, on the grounds that bureaucratic over-regulation leads to waste and inhibits enterprise. The first of these aims suggests a more tightly planned system with frequent checks on performance; the latter a shrivelling of central planning with institutions being encouraged to compete within a light regulatory framework. This tension has been highlighted by the inability of local education authorities to respond quickly and decisively enough to the challenge of falling rolls in secondary schools. Even under the terms of the 1944 Education Act, they possessed barely sufficient power to close and to amalgamate schools. The ability to appeal to the Secretary of State (at any rate in England and Wales) and the consequent delay before the Department of Education and Science reached its decision seriously compromised the planning powers of LEAs. Despite this they were frequently criticized by the National Audit Office and other bodies for failing to remove surplus school places from the system rapidly enough.

Under the terms of the Education Reform Act the powers of the LEAs have been further reduced: governing bodies are to be given greater discretion to manage the resources available to schools without reference to the wishes of LEAs; schools at odds with their LEAs will be able to opt out by applying for grant maintained status; and LEAs will no longer be able to limit pupil intakes to secure an even distribution of places across their schools. These measures certainly encourage, indeed oblige, schools to take more responsibility for their own management. But they also undermine efforts to make them more accountable. The same tension can be observed in relation to universities. On the one hand, they have come under greater surveillance by the Department of Education and Science (DES) and the UGC, in terms both of their detailed financial management and of their academic direction. These policies have been justified by the desire to make universities more accountable. On the other hand, they have been encouraged to strengthen their managerial processes and to engage in entrepreneurial activities. More recently it has been proposed that universities, and polytechnics and colleges of higher education, should be funded by means of state bursaries, or vouchers, paid direct to students, so avoiding the need for elaborate national planning. These alternative policies are justified by the wish to make universities more responsible for their own success or failure and less dependent on funds and directions from the government and its agents.

The [. . .] quality of responsiveness hovers uneasily between the other two. In some senses it is close to accountability, especially if responsiveness is defined in relation to political authority rather than market demand. At other times it is closer to responsibility, because only a responsible institution can be a responsive one. These difficulties – summed up by the question 'responsive to whom?' – will be discussed later in this chapter. For the moment, a simpler point is being emphasized, i.e. that these three qualities – accountability, responsiveness and responsibility – are by no means consistent with each other. So it is difficult to regard them as constituent parts of a common programme. They may arise from a common instinct, to open up the education system to outside influences, but they often result in contradictory policies.

Nevertheless, although care should be taken before associating the increasing interest in accountability, responsiveness and responsibility with the conservative tide that has been flowing through education since 1976 or in suggesting that they are compatible aspects of a common programme, it is important to discuss these trends in the wider policy context. They have been given renewed emphasis at a time when many progressive values and practices have come under attack. Inevitably this has coloured their presentation if not their substance. For example, this policy environment has encouraged a managerial rather than professional interpretation of responsiveness, while accountability has come to be seen more in terms of meeting market demands than of upholding cultural values.

Similarly, the inconsistencies between the policies designed to foster accountability, responsiveness and responsibility can be exaggerated. In a broad instinctive sense they do form a common programme. However diverse and centrifugal these policies, they perhaps have a common source, the desire to make education more accessible and relevant combined perhaps with a certain distrust of educators as professional experts and a measured disenchantment with the progressive ambitions typical of the 1960s. It is important to recognize this common source. Otherwise, the flavour of present discussions about accountability, responsiveness and responsibility may be lost.

This broader context also provides many disparate policies with a coherence they would otherwise lack. A whole tranche of policies that refer to accountability, responsiveness and responsibility, which have been developed since 1976, may appear at first sight a hopeless jumble. Increasing the number of parents on school governing bodies and giving those bodies greater independence from LEAs, stimulating competition between schools by requiring examination results to be published and allowing them to recruit up to their physical capacity, devolving financial and administrative powers to further education colleges, freeing polytechnics and colleges of higher education from local authority control, encouraging universities to raise more private income, replacing student grants with loans, publishing HMI reports on schools and colleges, even imposing a national curriculum – all of these policies possess an underlying coherence, not of course in the sense that they are administratively compatible, but in the sense that they all flow from a common critique of existing practices in education. This critique is that schools, colleges, polytechnics and universities are not sufficiently account-able, responsive and responsible.

So in discussing these three qualities it is important to strike a balance. To regard them simply as the outgrowth of a particular ideology is wrong. As important strands in educational policy they antedate any reaction against the progressive post-war consensus. Their significance also extends far beyond the political sphere. Accountability, responsiveness and responsi-bility must be regarded therefore as longstanding – even permanent – preoccupations within the education system. But it would be misleading not to acknowledge the influence of the particular context which has shaped the presentation of these preoccupations in the 1980s. As a result they are deeply ambiguous phenomena which require careful definition.

Accountability, responsiveness and responsibility are focused on the behaviour and performance of the institution, whether school or college. The wish to highlight these three particular aspects of the process of education and to emphasize the central role of the institution in promoting them is compara-tively recent. Until the 1970s accountability, responsiveness and responsi-bility were taken to be integral parts of the wider process of educating students which could not easily or sensibly be separated from the whole. They were regarded as part of the inner private life of the system, not of its political superstructure. Generally, they were placed in the context of educational purposes rather than of managerial outcomes. The institution was taken very much for granted. Charismatic leadership at institutional level was out of fashion, the relic of education's heroic age, although it was recognized that headteachers and principals were key figures in establishing high standards and morale. But the emphasis was not so much on the institution as on the micro-relationships between pupils and students and their teachers and the macro-relationships between the education system, society and the economy. The institution was not necessarily seen as having any significant potency of its own, still less any moral worth.

The situation today is different. Both responsiveness, flanked by accountability and responsibility, and institutions are the subject of increas-ing emphasis, the former because doubts, already discussed, have been raised about the responsiveness of education and the latter because the institution has come to be seen by many as a 'missing link', the key to integrity, quality, relevance, community and many other characteristics which are felt to be lacking in modern education. The emphasis on both has also been increased by the long march of managerialism through British education. University vice-chancellors and polytechnic directors are encouraged to regard themselves as chief executives of large enterprises. Departments within these institutions have been redesignated as cost centres. Headteachers in schools, assisted by their governing bodies, are to be made responsible for managing their own resources. Further education colleges must bid for contracts to provide training places funded by the Training Agency (formerly the Manpower Services Commission). There are many other examples of managerialism in British education today. Much of it, of course, is rhetoric; it relabels rather than rewrites existing relationships. But some of it is of substantial significance.

Reasons for the managerial revolution

There are two main reasons for the rise of managerialism. The first is largely political – or perhaps structural would be a more appropriate adjective. In education, as in most other areas of social policy, more must be done with less. The curriculum in schools has become more sophisticated and, although the imposition of a national curriculum may act as a brake on variety, the pressure to incorporate new skills and new knowledge into the curriculum will be remorseless. More pupils are encouraged to stay on at school or college after the minimum leaving age of 16. Those who leave despite such encouragement are provided with increasingly elaborate (although not necessarily effective!) youth training programmes. Those who stay are offered increased opportunities to enter higher education. Pre-school and nursery education have also been expanded. Few people object to these advances in education, which are generally supposed to be inescapable in an open society and an advanced economy. But they cost a great deal of money. Until the 1980s expenditure on education in Britain consistently increased at a much faster rate than the gross national product; during the 1980s intermittently so. Many governments, including the present British one, have attempted to restrain the growth of public expenditure. The reasons for this, and their validity, fall outside the scope of this chapter. But the restriction of public expenditure at a time when other social and economic demands have forced the education system to become increasingly elaborate has largely determined the context in which educational policy must be made. A responsible institution must be at the same time responsive to new educational needs, which means spending more, and accountable to government and local authorities, which means spending less.

So the growing elaboration and sophistication of education push costs up; government tries to curb these rising costs. The inevitable result has been pressure on institutions to be more cost-effective, in the sense of maximizing the use of scarcer resources, and more efficient, in the sense of reducing unit costs. The only way in which most institutions can become more cost-effective and efficient, without of course limiting the scope or cutting the quality of their services, is to strengthen their management. Tough and often unpopular decisions have to be taken, new opportunities have to be seized, new markets developed. Sadly, it may be true that in the past many schools and colleges were under-managed, or rather that their management structure and style had been designed for a different environment, the expansion of systems still rooted in élitist attitudes and practices at a time when resources were plentiful and social and economic demands less volatile. Today's environment is more populist, less prosperous, more uncertain. So management styles have had to change. It is probably not reasonable to object to this change. In an important sense it is as much a sympton of success as of decline. Large, complex institutions with diverse roles must be more deliberately managed than small, simple ones with restricted roles. The managerial revolutions in schools, colleges and universities is perhaps a growing pain of a mature educational system. If that revolution has thrown into sharper relief the issue of accountability, responsiveness and responsibility, it is no loss.

The second reason for the long march of managerialism is more ideological. [. . .] There are those who argue that the managerial revolution in British education is about much more than discovering and disseminating the best management practice. It is also an attempt to replace, or at any rate subordinate, professional and collegial values that have always been important in education. So notions of line management are to be substituted for those of professional responsibility. The aim of the managerial revolution, therefore, should be not only to improve the cost-effectiveness and efficiency of schools and colleges but to modify their system of values. The changes in management style then become a metaphor for more significant changes in the very process of education – from liberal to utilitarian, from student-centred learning to skills-based training, from critical to conformist values, from humanity to technocracy.

In practice, it is difficult to distinguish between structural and ideological reasons. For example, it can be argued that collegial management based on professional solidarity inhibits the most efficient operation of an institution. So it must be disbanded, or modified, not because it is wrong in essence but because it stands in the way of progress. An extension of this argument, although with a more pronounced ideological flavour, is that professors, lecturers and teachers represent a producers' cartel. So they must be dethroned in the cause of consumer sovereignty. A third argument is that private enterprises are better managed than public institutions. So the management practices of the former must be imposed on the latter. Of course there are private sector practices that could profitably be imitated in education, as there are the other way round. But the style of management must relate both to the mission and to the economy of an institution. This is as important because there may be a crude desire to impose on education patterns of governance and administration that are not appropriate. The contrast here is between process and goals. Many, but not all, private enterprises must manage processes more complex than those in schools and colleges (but not perhaps universities and polytechnics). But their goals, even in the cases of large multinational companies, are generally straightforward. Because schools and colleges must balance a series of demands – for democratic accountability, for professional autonomy, for student satisfaction – their management has to be more elaborate and even opaque than that of equivalently sized enterprises outside the system.

Responsiveness and accountability distinguished

A totally satisfactory definition of responsiveness is, of course, impossible. It is sometimes seen as the culmination and the justification of this managerial revolution in schools and colleges and therefore as a virtual synonym for accountability. But for reasons which have already been discussed, this is too casual an approximation. Responsiveness describes the willingness of an institution – or, indeed, an individual – to respond on its or their own initiative, i.e. the capacity to be open to outside impulses and new ideas. Accountability, in contrast, describes the submission of the institution or individual to a form of external audit, its capacity to account for its or their own performance. So they are different ideas. Responsiveness is freely arrived at; accountability is imposed from outside. Of course, under modern conditions it is difficult to imagine a responsive institution that is not also an accountable institution. But the first concept subsumes the second – it is a much broader idea.

Four aspects of responsiveness

Although it is important to bear in mind this important distinction between responsiveness and accountability, it is pedantic to insist on their complete separation. In the context of education the two must be discussed together. Four aspects of this combined, and therefore complex, concept deserve to be discussed: the first two relate more particularly to the idea of accountability and the second two to the broader notion of responsiveness.

The first aspect is that of political accountability. It is a reasonable argument that in an open and democratic society the government must be sovereign. All institutions, and especially those supported largely by public expenditure like schools or universities, should be subject to its ultimate will. A popularly elected government has an authority and legitimacy superior to all others. That at any rate is the theory, and increasingly the practice too, of what passes for the British constitution.

This theory of course is not beyond all challenge. First, it is not the government *per se* that is sovereign but the people. The idea of the natural rights of citizens is at the root of democracy. Therefore, acts of government that tend to diminish their rights cannot be made legitimate because they are apparently endorsed by an electoral majority. Education of course is bound up with some powerful natural rights – of parents, of free intellectual inquiry, of critical freedom. These rights logically should set limits to the power of the government in education. It cannot be all powerful. Of course, if the idea of responsiveness to the state, in the wider sense of the whole community along with its inherited intellectual and cultural traditions, is substituted for a narrow accountability to a particular government, a different picture emerges. In this wider perspective the educational system helps to form the state as well as being an important component of it. But this distinction between state and government can only be maintained under conditions of consensual politics such as have not been enjoyed in Britain for more than a decade.

This is not the place to speculate on a democratic theory of education. But one other inhibition on the government's authority over education must be mentioned. From the earliest childhood years to the advanced frontiers of science the process of education is founded on rationality. This commitment to rationality must be reflected in the system's own organization and management. Reasonable decisions, in administrative as well as intellectual matters, rest on the sophistication rather than the simplification of knowledge. Yet any government which attempts to plan education in detail must depend on simplified knowledge. It is possible to concentrate power but not knowledge. Therefore, education may be in a special position in relation to political authority because its mission is to teach skills and to transmit and renew knowledge, tasks not amenable to political direction.

These arguments may suggest that even democratic governments should be allowed little power over education. But there are two senses in which schools and colleges must be accountable to government. First, because the system is largely supported by public funds, it must be accountable in a managerial sense for the best possible use of those funds. Secondly, government has a right and even a duty to determine the broad character of the schools and colleges which it supports so that they contribute fully to economic development, social progress, cultural conservation, individual fulfilment and other goals which enjoy widespread support. It seems reasonable, therefore, to allow governments to decide whether secondary schools should be organized according to a comprehensive or selective pattern or whether entry to higher education should be restricted or open.

The second aspect is that of market accountability. Here the role of the customer, whether student or employer, is emphasized. If only the customer, according to this argument, can be placed in a direct relationship with the supplier of the services they seek, then a self-regulatory market can be allowed to operate. Both choice and efficiency will be maximized without the need for ugly political interventions. But three important qualifications tend to compromise the ingenious symmetry of a market model of accountability and responsiveness. The first is the obvious difficulty of definition – who is the customer? The pupil or student or their parents? If the interests of the first are regarded as paramount, who is best able to interpret them? Their parents? Their teachers? The government in some form? Or it may be argued that the government is the real customer so long as education is largely tax-supported. These questions are both philosophical and logistical. Their complexity and ambiguity undermine the idea of the 'hidden hand' of the market in education.

The second qualification is that, in nearly every case, it is a managed not a free market. The education system's position as a near-monopoly supplier is maintained by a range of regulations – compulsory attendance at school, the qualification and registration of professional workers such as teachers, doctors and lawyers, and so on. A free market would require all these controls to be lifted. But this of course would inevitably undermine notions of quality that are central to the process of education. However, the difficulty is not simply with supply; it is also with demand. On grounds of equity, access to schools and colleges could not be limited by the ability to pay. As a result any government interested in promoting market accountability would need to devise a scheme of entitlement, or 'vouchers', that could be used to 'buy' education. But any restriction on the availability of or eligibility for 'vouchers', or on where they could be spent, would rig the market, rather as the present system of student support does in higher education.

The third qualification concerns the external benefits that accrue to society from education which cannot be attributed to particular individuals. To take the simplest example, a person's value to society or the economy is not necessarily or even arguably the same as the value of their individual recompense in the form of wages or salaries. Or, to ask a straightforward question, how can investment in maintaining and expanding a society's cultural capital be attributed as benefits to particular consumers of education? For education is not a single good, but many. In one sense it is firmly non-positional, valuable in its own right. In another sense it is a positional good, its value fluctuating according to its availability. It is both an intensely private experience and a public commodity to be traded in the skills market. As a result of this complexity, education is resistant to a market version of accountability. As is the case with political accountability, market account-ability can only be made to work by drastically simplifying the process and indeed the essence of education.

The third aspect of responsiveness is that of professional responsibility. In some ways this is an alternative form of accountability to the market mechanism which has just been discussed. No one seriously argues that teachers, doctors or engineers, or the institutions which educate them, should be unaccountable to those they ultimately serve. But it may be that this essential accountability is best captured within a web of professional obligations. For such obligations are not external constraints that can be justly resented. Instead, they embody codes of practice and sets of values that are all the more influential because they are self-imposed. If responsiveness is looked at through the lens of professional responsibility, there is less need to worry about the identity of the customer. Those with a properly professional outlook know that it is the student or the patient who must be served not those who sign the cheques. There is also less need to worry about external benefits. True professionals know that they are members of a wider corporation of practitioners which embodies both tradition and progress. Of course, a sense of professional responsibility cannot be relied on exclusively to secure responsiveness today. Professions are often conservative and try to exclude new ways of thinking and working, and indeed new people. There are examples in the law and medicine where professionals' *esprit de corps* may have distorted the direction of change or acted as a barrier to innovation. Other professions, in contrast, are weak and disorganized, and therefore unable to take over a leading role in the definition of responsiveness. School if not university teaching may be an example. But in discussing ways to improve the responsiveness of institutions and individuals in education it would be wrong to ignore the professional model. It does allow accountability to be exercised outside the immediate context of politics and the market.

The fourth aspect is that of cultural responsibility, the allegiance to rationality, truth and knowledge, which all those engaged in education must accept. Perhaps their first and last responsibility is to these things – the good, the true and the beautiful as understood by the ancient Greeks. Indeed, this may be the ultimate form of responsiveness. Real change in education comes from new insights, new knowledge, new understanding. An institution that fails to foster such things or an individual who has little regard for them can hardly be regarded as responsive. To be responsive in such terms an institution or individual must be critical, and the capacity to be critical may require some insulation from the insistent pressures of politics and the market. This is not a popular argument in Britain at present because it sounds like a justification of unaccountability and even irresponsibility. This is not necessarily so. Education at all levels must be responsible in this primary and fundamental sense before its accountability to the state, the market or society can have any substantial significance. For without this primary responsiveness education would be truly a dead world. Its external utility is rooted in its internal validity, its private integrity.

The effect of this discussion may have been to obscure rather than to illuminate the idea of responsiveness in schools and colleges. That was not the intention; it is merely a reflection of the complexity and subtlety of the concept. Accountability and responsibility are both parts of responsiveness but they need to be carefully distinguished. The various layers of responsiveness – the political, the market, the professional and the cultural – also need to be distinguished. The danger is that a simple-minded, one-dimensional, tough-talking definition of responsiveness in education will be adopted. There may be those who feel they have found the entire answer in democratic accountability; others in the free market. They believe in a single key, a philosopher's stone. Perhaps such an approach grows out of the irritation at the inwardness of education which has stimulated the growing interest in accountability, responsiveness and responsibility. But the other, and more sensible, view of responsiveness is that it is necessarily multidimensional because education serves so many groups – students, parents, employers, society, culture, even history itself – and because it has to balance the interests of these competing groups within working institutions.

Institutions: Their 'public' and 'private' lives

Institutions in education of course lead a double life. They are both administrative and moral entities. In recent years attention has been concentrated on the first of these aspects. The apotheosis (or perhaps the reverse!) of this view of institutions is summed up in the American characterization of a university as a collection of individuals and departments held together by a common grievance over car parking. Radicals on both left and right have tended to be dismissive of institutions. Student radicals of the 1960s and 1970s saw them as embodying the hegemony of a stifling materialistic bourgeoisie. Free-market radicals of the 1980s have tended to regard institutions as cartels, arthritic bureaucratic structures that block the free flow of consumer choice. Older-fashioned conservatives have often seen them as mechanistic and amoral, organizations obsessed with administration that have grown far away from their informing intentions. Perhaps only the centre-left has had much good to say for institutions.

But this essentially negative view of institutions must be challenged, especially when they are the carriers of powerful social and cultural values as they are in education. For students and pupils the university or the school is their experiential world. The significance of the institution should not be underestimated for at least three reasons. First, education is about far more than what happens in the classroom or the lecture theatre. The 'hidden curriculum' of the playground or the 'black economy' of the students' union may be as decisive an experience as the formal curriculum.

Secondly, an important factor in producing high-quality education is the quality of institutional life, the ethos of an institution. The headteacher or, in further and higher education, the head of department, is a key figure in determining quality. The institution is an area in which charismatic leadership, which is once again respected, can be exercised. Of course, the institution, like the responsiveness it encourages, is an obscure category. In this moral context it is certainly smaller than the university or polytechnic which under modern conditions are condemned to live an almost exclusively bureaucratic life. It is probably larger than a single department in a secondary school, which perhaps lacks the independent authority to act as this kind of moral focus. There is room for considerable debate on this question. But if the institution is regarded as a moral entity rather than simply as a bureaucratic organization, questions of size and issues of devolution acquire considerable importance. Almost too much is known about the 'public life' of institutions – how they should be planned, managed, funded and organized – and too little is understood about their 'private life' – how they work to educate people, how they successfully transmit social and cultural values, how they model the conduct of modern society. Yet it is in this second context, of institutions as moral entities, that the most important issues of accountability, responsiveness and responsibility arise.

The third reason for emphasizing the moral as well as the administrative aspect of institutions is more speculative. In modern industrial societies the individual is often isolated, one among millions of voters or consumers. They are confronted and absorbed by their own private relationships while the state, in a wider sense than simply the government, is increasingly powerful. There is therefore an urgent need to create and to sustain mediating institutions that bring together these chaotic private and alien public worlds. This was what De Tocqueville admired about early nineteenth-century America, the abundance of voluntary and local associations, churches, clubs, societies, townships and, of course, schools, which sustained the civic virtue of that nation. Of course, in the United States the school has always been regarded as a moral instrument, a place where new Americans are made and where private and public worlds collide. But in Britain the same need exists. Education, both as a responsive process and as a set of mediating institutions, has a key role to play in fulfilling our democracy, in welding together the fractures in modern culture.

Here is the heart of accountability, responsiveness and responsibility, a surprisingly long way from the territory of performance indicators, external audits and other such devices which is conventionally taken to be where they belong.

2
Organizations, technology and environment

Lee G. Bolman and Terrence E. Deal

Technology and environment

What determines the shape of an organization's structure? Why are Harvard University and McDonald's structured so differently, even though each is viewed as a very effective organization? Current research points to technology and environment as the two most powerful factors in influencing how an organization is structured.

Technology

The technology of an organization is its central activity for transforming inputs into outputs. Although the word *technology* usually evokes images of machinery and hardware, the concept is broader than that. In schools, the basic technology is classroom teaching. In medicine, technology includes the many activities that physicians perform to diagnose and treat illness. In social service agencies, the basic technology is 'casework' – a series of encounters between the caseworker and the client.

Technology in organizations has been conceptualized in a number of ways. Dornbusch and Scott (1975), for example, identify three forms of technology. 'Materials' technology is the concrete, human or symbolic materials that form the organization's inputs. 'Operations' technology consists of the activities for transforming raw materials into desired ends. 'Knowledge' technology comprises the underlying beliefs about cause and effect that link materials, activity and outcomes. Schools, hospitals, factories, prisons, political organizations and churches all rely on technologies to transform materials, people or ideas from one state to another.

Technologies differ in their clarity, predictability and effectiveness. The technology for assembling an automobile or manufacturing an electric mixer is relatively routine and programmed. The task is clear, most of the potential problems are known in advance, and the probability of successful manufacture is known and assured. Other technologies are much less routine and predictable. In teaching, for example, the day's objectives can be complicated and amorphous; students' needs and skills vary widely; their moods fluctuate in response to weather, time of day, or an immediate distraction; knowing what approach will work with a particular student is often very difficult. In surgery the clarity of the task varies with the difficulty of the procedure. Appendectomies are fairly straightforward, but heart transplants are much less routine. Something can go wrong with any surgical procedure, though, simply because the human body is so complex. The success or failure of an operation can depend on a host of postoperative conditions, including the attitudes of the patient's family, the nursing care, diet, and the presence or absence of numerous complications.

Environment

Environment is typically seen as everything outside the boundaries of an organization, even though the boundaries are often nebulous and poorly drawn. It is the environment that provides raw materials to an organization and receives the organization's outputs. Businesses procure materials and resources from the environment and distribute products or services to customers or clients. Schools receive students from the local community and later return graduates to the community.

The nature of an organization's environment can vary on a number of dimensions. Scott (1981), for example, focuses on the dimensions of uncertainty and dependence. Organizational environments are uncertain when they are diverse, unstable and unpredictable. Organizations with rapidly changing technologies or markets – for instance, high-technology electronics corporations – must cope with high degrees of environmental uncertainty. A new state-of-the-art product may be outmoded in six months. Any organization that finds itself in rapidly changing economic or political conditions also deals with high levels of uncertainty. In contrast, a stable, mature business such as a railroad or a post office department deals with much lower environmental uncertainty. Organizations that face high uncertainty need high levels of flexibility and adaptability to cope and are likely to be less bureaucratic and more decentralized. A well-known example is Digital Equipment Corporation, a fast-growing manufacturer of minicomputers. Historically, Digital had no organization charts, paid little attention to job titles, and encouraged creative entrepreneurship in its employees. (A representative of the major industry magazines called Digital to check on the title of one of its executives and was surprised to learn that the company was not sure what his title was and did not care because it would probably change soon anyway.) As the company matured and growth began to slow, Digital went through a period of reappraisal, and pressures to tighten up began to appear.

Different parts of the same organization may face very different environments. Lawrence and Lorsch (1967) found that, in the plastics industry, uncertainty was much higher for the research and development departments than for manufacturing, and sales was somewhere between the two. They found corresponding differences in the way each of those functions was organized in the most effective plastics firms. It was only in the ineffective firms that the organization had not found a way to develop different structures for the three functions.

All organizations are dependent on their environment, but the degree of dependence varies. Some organizations have very low power with respect to their environment, and it is difficult for them to get the resources they need. Organizations are likely to be dependent if they are relatively small, if they are surrounded by more powerful competitors or well-organized constituencies, and if they have little flexibility and few slack resources in responding to environmental fluctuations. An organization like Harvard University is insulated from its environment by size, élite status and a large endowment. A small private college with no endowment is much more dependent on the fluctuations and expectations of the environment. Harvard can afford to give low teaching loads and high freedom to its faculty. A small college with serious financial pressures is likely to have tighter controls, higher work loads and limited discretion. Harvard can afford to maintain substantial academic programs in classical Greek and Latin even if most of the courses are under-enrolled. The poorer college will be forced to eliminate anything that does not attract students and pay its own way.

Relationships among structure, technology, and environment

The structure of an organization is influenced by, and often influences, its technology and environment. The mutual relationship among the three has led to the development of 'contingency theories'. Those theories argue that effective organizations develop structures to match the demands or needs of technologies and environments. There is no one best way to organize, because a workable structure for one combination of technology and environment may be inappropriate for another. The key to organizational effectiveness is to tailor the structure to fit the situation.

Two major examples of contingency theory (Lawrence and Lorsch, 1967; Galbraith, 1977) both focus on one basic idea – the structure of an organization depends particularly on the amount of *uncertainty* the organization has to deal with. Organizations that live in relatively simple, stable environments can develop relatively simple, stable structures. Organizations that live in turbulent, changing, uncertain environments need structures that are more complex, differentiated and flexible.

Lawrence and Lorsch studied organizations in three industries: box containers, foods and plastics. The container industry is a slow-growth sector in which the main objectives are consistent quality and prompt service. Innovation is not emphasized, because proven containers produced rapidly and at low cost give organizations a competitive edge. The packaged foods industry is in a more rapidly changing environment; innovative marketing approaches are a major factor in success. Plastics, in the 1960s, was a rapidly changing, high-growth environment. The dominant competitive issue was the development and introduction of new and revised products.

Each industry had a different environment and relied on different technologies. Lawrence and Lorsch discussed three major dimensions of the task environment: clarity of information, uncertainty of cause-and-effect relations, and the time-span for feedback. When information is unclear, knowledge is limited and feedback is slow, an organization has to deal with very high levels of uncertainty.

Lawrence and Lorsch believed that environmental uncertainty would have a major impact on four major organizational characteristics: the degree of formality and bureaucracy in the structure, how people related to each other, how people dealt with time, and what goals the organization sought.

They reasoned that it is much easier for an organization to have accurate information about its environment if the environment is stable. Jobs can be specified through predetermined rules. Communications can be handled through the formal channels. A straightforward, task-oriented managerial style is likely to be effective.

If the environment is complex and rapidly changing, the task is more difficult. Rules may be outmoded as soon as they are made. The organization needs more points of contact with the environment, so a flatter hierarchy is needed. Much more information needs to be communicated, and the traditional channels cannot handle all of it, so that a much more complex, multiple-channel communications system is needed. Such a system is likely to work better with an interpersonal style that emphasizes building effective relationships.

Lawrence and Lorsch added an additional element – in most large organizations, different subunits face different environments. In the plastics industry, the research units face much more uncertainty than the manufacturing units. If the two units are structured the same way, at least one of them will have a poor fit with its own task environment. In order for the research and the manufacturing departments each to do its own job well, the two departments need different structures and different management styles. The more diverse the environments that different units face, the more differentiation in structure is needed.

But as differentiation increases, integration becomes more difficult. The more different two units are, the harder it will be for them to work together. A researcher with a long time orientation may become very frustrated with a manufacturing manager who rarely thinks more than a day or so into the future. If an organization has little internal differentiation, then rules, procedures and hierarchy may provide sufficient integration. But if an organization has high uncertainty and diversity, then task forces, integrating units, co-ordinators and more face-to-face interaction become necessary.

Lawrence and Lorsch's research generally confirmed their theory. Within industries, organizations with structures that fit the environment were found to be more effective. Effective container organizations were more centralized and formalized than effective plastics organizations. The effective plastics firms had higher levels of differentiation and more complex approaches to integration.

Galbraith (1977) also viewed uncertainty as central in determining organizational structure. He defined uncertainty as the difference between the information that an organization already has and the information that it needs. How much it needs depends on three things: the diversity of its output, the diversity of its input (which Galbraith measured in terms of the number of specialities included within the organization), and the level of goal difficulty. As uncertainty increases, more information is needed to make decisions – information that the organization may not have. For simple, predictable tasks, an organization can plan in advance how things are to be handled. But planning is harder when uncertainty is high, and decisions have to be made as the task moves along.

As uncertainty increases, Galbraith argues, organizations are confronted with two choices: either reduce the need for information processing or increase the capacity to process information. Organizations can reduce information processing by creating slack resources or by creating self-contained units that can work on their own without depending on other units in the organization. If each project in a research firm is given its own editor instead of relying on one editorial department, the organization has created a slack resource (more editors than it needs) and made each department more self-contained. By spending more money on editors, the organization reduces the need for researchers to spend time coordinating with the editorial department.

An organization can increase its capacity to process information by investing in vertical information systems (computers and personnel to collect information and direct it to decision makers) or by developing lateral relations (direct contacts, liaison roles, project teams and matrix structures).

As organizations face more complicated tasks, they must choose one or a combination of the strategies. If no choice is made, slack resources are automatically created and organizational costs increase. But each of the strategies has costs as well as benefits.

Lawrence and Lorsch and Galbraith share the view that effective organizations are those that build structures to meet technological and environmental demands. Both focus on the role of uncertainty and the way it affects the information needs of organizations. Both argue that simpler, more 'bureaucratic' organizations are most likely to be effective in relatively stable, predictable environments, whereas environments that are turbulent and uncertain breed more complex organizational structures.

References

Dornbusch, S. M. and Scott, W. R. (1975). *Evaluation and the Exercise of Authority: A Theory of Control Applied to Diverse Organizations*. San Francisco, Jossey-Bass.

Galbraith, J. (1977). *Organization Design*. Reading, Mass., Addison-Wesley.

Lawrence, P. and Lorsch, J. (1967). *Organization and Environment*. Boston, Division of Research, Harvard Business School.

Scott, W. R. (1981). *Organizations: Rational, Natural, and Open Systems*. Englewood Cliffs, N.J., Prentice-Hall.

3

Schools and their external environments

Wayne K. Hoy and Cecil G. Miskel

In the classical management and human relations perspectives, organizations are viewed as relatively closed systems. The dominant metaphor is that organizations can be understood as simple machines. Efficient internal operations are thought to determine effectiveness. Those early perspectives assume organizational and administrative policies are designed to fulfil a relatively stable set of tasks and goals; therefore, little attention is given to how organizations adapt to their external environments. In contrast, contemporary thought about organizations assumes a much broader view. William L. Boyd and Robert L. Crowson observe that the continuing environmental turbulence of the 1960s showed that a closed-systems model was not adequate for either illuminating or dealing with the pressing problems of educational administrators.[1]* As a result of the search for more practically relevant models, organizations such as school systems are now viewed as open systems, which must adapt to changing external conditions to be effective and, in the long term, survive.[2] The open-system concept highlights the vulnerability and interdependence of organizations and their environments. In other words, environment is important because it affects the internal structures and processes of organizations; hence, one is forced to look both inside and outside the organization to explain organizational behavior.

Although the environments of some schools and districts may be relatively simple and stable, most tend to be complex and dynamic. Indeed, the larger social, economic, political and technological trends all tend to influence the internal operations of schools and districts. Because school organizations are conceptualized as part of a larger universe or environment,

* Superscript numerals refer to numbered notes at the end of this chapter.

an argument can be made that anything that happens in the larger environment may affect the school and vice versa. For example, one only needs to observe the race by school districts to purchase personal computers for instructional purposes to see the effects that recent technology and its projected economic benefits for society have had on the internal processes of schools.

Environment, like a number of other terms in organizational theory, is not a firmly defined concept. Consensus neither exists about what constitutes an organization's environment, nor the essential issues to be considered in discussions of organizational environment.[3] Nevertheless, similar definitions, common elements or dimensions, and information and resource dependence perspectives all provide useful descriptions and explanations of school environments.[4]

Defining organizational environment

Numerous definitions of organizational environment occur in the literature. Four examples follow:

> Environment is typically seen as everything outside the boundaries of an organization, even though the boundaries are often nebulous and poorly drawn.[5]

> Organizational environment is all elements existing outside the boundary of the organization that have the potential to affect all or part of the organization.[6]

> In a general sense, the environment of a system consists of 'everything else' – that is everything that is not-system.[7]

> The *external environment* consists of those relevant physical and social factors *outside* the boundaries of the organization . . . that are taken into consideration in the decision-making behavior of individuals in that system.[8]

A common theme of these definitions is that environment is treated as a residual category of potential and real effects. Defining environment as a residual component of school organizations may be sufficient when the focus of attention is on the internal processes of the school itself, but not when treating the environment as a causal force that is influencing the structure and activities of schools.[9] As a consequence, environment and its effects on the internal aspects of the organization can be understood by defining and analyzing its most salient dimensions.

Dimensions of environments

A distinction between general and specific environments provides an initial clarification of the environment as a residual category.[10] Broad factors,

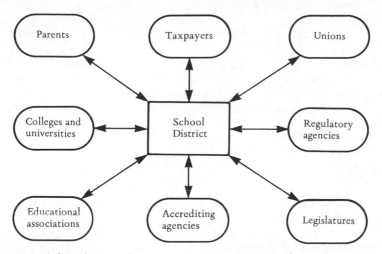

Figure 3.1 Selected external constituencies for school districts.

trends and conditions that can potentially affect organizations comprise the general environment of schools. Examples include technological and informational developments, political structures and patterns of legal norms, social conditions and cultural values, economic factors, and ecological and demographic characteristics. Although the potential exists for general factors to influence a given school or district, their relevance and likelihood of impact are not entirely clear to the organization's members. In other words, ambiguity and uncertainty exist about the effects of the general environment on any specific school.

In contrast, external factors that have immediate and direct effects on organizations are termed the specific environment. As shown in Fig. 3.1, specific environmental factors for school districts include constituencies and stakeholders such as individual parents, taxpayer associations, teacher and administrator unions, state and federal government regulatory agencies, colleges and universities, state legislatures, accrediting agencies, and other associations involved in educational policies and practices (e.g. Parent–Teachers Associations and groups for handicapped or gifted children and athletic and art programs).

The general environment is similar for all organizations. Depending on the particular circumstances, however, specific environments vary from school to school and from district to district. Administrators tend to focus the monitoring and planning processes on specific environmental elements and often fail to recognize that general environmental factors have the potential to influence not only the organization itself, but the specific environments as well. During the 1970s, for instance, the oil pricing policies of the OPEC cartel not only tripled or quadrupled the price of utilities for schools but triggered a rapid inflationary cycle that had severe consequences for other school costs. Different aspects of the general environment also interact with each other. For example, political decisions and social attitudes combined to

create civil disobedience in educational institutions during the Vietnam War
era of the 1960s and early 1970s.

Thus, external environments of schools are complex and difficult
to analyze, but an enhanced understanding may be gained by examining
general characteristics of the environment. Three dimensions – uncertainty,
clustering and scarcity – are particularly useful.

Uncertainty

Fundamentally, the *degree of uncertainty* involves informational aspects of the
environment. The level of uncertainty is determined by the kind and amount
of information that organizational decision makers have about trends and
changes in environmental conditions. Uncertainty is viewed as a problematic
situation confronting organizations. Thus, in conditions of high uncertainty,
alternative decisions and their outcomes become increasingly unpredictable
and risky.

Stability and complexity affect environmental uncertainty. Stability
refers to the extent to which elements in the environment are undergoing
change. Stable environments experience little change, whereas unstable
environments experience abrupt and rapid changes. Stability occurs in
situations where the set of important elements remains constant and are either
unchanging or changing slowly and predictably. Instability arises in situations that are loose and erratic. In conditions of instability, both the value and
kinds of environmental elements are changing unpredictably.[11] Instability
produces uncertainty.

Complexity refers to the number and similarity of environmental
elements to which the organization must relate. A complex environment has
a large number of diverse entities that exert significant influence on the
organization, whereas a simple environment is relatively homogeneous and
characterized by only a few important external elements. In other words,
environments with many diverse and important elements are highly complex. In schools, for example, the number and types of special education
populations that must be served would be one indicator of the complexity of a
school's environment.

Less complex environments are less uncertain. Fewer important information categories are necessary for decision making; beliefs about cause
and effect relations are more certain; and preferences regarding possible
outcomes are more clear. Furthermore, when environmental elements are
similar, the range of expected behavior, strategies and tactics, and formal
goals are relatively easy to understand and handle. In contrast, highly
complex environments present memory problems for administrators and
organizations.[12] Moreover, causal relationships and preferences for possible
outcomes are more uncertain.

The more complex and unstable the environment, the greater the
uncertainty for the organization. Schools, like all formal organizations, need

determinateness and certainty because they are subject to the criteria of rationality. Hence, schools when confronted with uncertainty will often attempt to cope by creating special parts specifically to deal with it.[13] School districts, for example, develop special units such as offices of public relations to monitor the activities of significant groups in the environment and routinely report their behaviors and attitudes to the administrators.

Clustering

Environments differ in the *degree of clustering* or structuring as compared to anarchy or randomness.[14] At the highly clustered end of this dimension, environments present any organization with a powerful and highly structured set of demands and constraints. The price of survival is compliance; organizations such as schools which deviate too much from the requirements and values of the environment are altered or destroyed. At the other end of the continuum, poorly organized environments lack order, which makes further diversity to be tolerated easily. For example, a school policy might be in conflict with a given aspect of an unclustered community, but the deviance would not be construed as a general or intolerable breach of values. In a clustered community, however, the serious conflict might well produce a strong reaction from highly structured and interconnected community groups.

Scarcity

The *degree of scarcity* is the extent to which the environment has the resources available to support stability and sustained growth of the organization. For example, does the school district have resources to maintain a comprehensive program for the number of students in a school attendance area? Daniel Katz and Robert L. Kahn observe that, as the environment of an organization is examined for available resources, the dimension of scarcity becomes extremely important.[15] The relative abundance of resources in the specific and general environments is the ultimate determinant of sufficient input for any organization. The concept of abundance applies to informational and technical knowledge, economic and human resources, and political and legal support. Under conditions of scarcity, competition for resources among sub-groups can take the form of a zero-sum game with each sub-group caring more about its share of finite resources than the overall welfare of the organization. When student enrollments are declining, for instance, administrators may deny student transfers to needed programs in other schools because the action would decrease the human resource base of their schools.

Information perspective

The information perspective assumes the environment is a source of information that is used by decision makers as a basis for maintaining or changing internal structures and processes.[16] A primary concern of this approach is the degree of uncertainty of information reaching the organization's decision makers. A general assumption is made that decision-making processes are affected both by environmental uncertainty and the equivocal nature of the information generated by unstable and complex environments. An important tenet is that *perception* of information is assumed to be an intervening link between the organization's environment and actions taken by decision makers. Therefore, organizational environment consists of perceived information about the dimensions rather than objective descriptions of the elements themselves. In other words, the information perspective defines environment as the perceptions of external dimensions by organizational decision makers and other participants based on questionable and suspicious communications.

Specific formulations and empirical tests of the information perspective of organizational environments have typically been based on typologies using the dimensions of uncertainty and clustering. We will focus our analysis on four useful typologies that have been the object of considerable attention by organizational theorists.

Typologies of environments

Emery and Trist developed a now classic four-category typology of organizational environments using uncertainty and clustering.[17] They introduced the concept of 'causal texture' to indicate that environmental elements represent threats or opportunities for the organization. Four causal textures or environmental categories were proposed by Emery and Trist: placid, randomized; placid, clustered; disturbed, reactive; and turbulent field. Each type of causal texture represents a different combination of uncertainty and clustering.

Placid, randomized environments are the simplest type. Placid means that the relatively few important specific factors change slowly, and new threats or opportunities are infrequent. The environment is random or unclustered because when change does occur it is not predictable and it is not coordinated with other environmental elements. In other words, placid, randomized environments are relatively unchanging, with limited interdependence among specific factors or parts. Thus, the environment poses little threat to the organization.

An example is a small school district in a stable rural community. Years can pass without abrupt changes. Students, teachers and administrators come from families who have deep roots in the area. Other than an occasional church group and an athletic booster club, few special interest groups make systematic attempts to influence the school. Events that might have a major impact on the district are unlikely. In this kind of environment, the professional staff can concentrate on the day-to-day operations of the school.

The environment typically is not a major factor in the administrators' decision making.

Placid, clustered environments are relatively stable, but increased interdependence or growing complexity is evident. Specific elements in the environment are coupled to one another and may act simultaneously to influence the organization. Events in the environment are not random. When threats or opportunities appear, they come from organized clusters, which may be potentially dangerous to the organization. Because a number of factors may change simultaneously, planning and forecasting processes are important and day-to-day operations should allow for possible new events in the environment.

An example is the environment experienced by a moderate to large school district in a stable community setting. In such a community, the number of specific elements not only would be large but would be linked together through a dominant industry, labor union, informal power structure, civic organization or religious group. When threats or opportunities appear for the school district, they will come at the same time from a united or organized set of specific environmental elements. The dominant industry might decide to introduce a new product line or expand operations. As a direct request, company officials themselves would personally ask school officials to introduce new vocational education programs to assist the economic growth of the firm and community. As an indirect approach, allied groups such as labor unions and other business groups would reinforce the need for the new programs.

Disturbed, reactive environments are dynamic and exhibit changes that are not random. Actions by one organization can disturb the environment and provoke reactions by others. The disturbed, reactive environment is comprised of organizations of the same kind that are competing for domination of a particular segment of the market. Each competing organization attempts to improve its own conditions by hindering the other, each knowing the others are playing the same game.

In education, the disturbed, reactive environment is a community with competing school districts, for example, public and private, each wanting to dominate. The role of administrators in this type of environment is to plan decisions and strategic moves to allow for countermoves. If a private school is claiming high academic achievement and orderly procedures, the planning by administrators in other schools must consider not only its response but the reactions of all school organizations in the community. Administrators must carefully monitor other groups and prepare alternative actions to their moves. This type of environment may not be widespread today in the United States, but other countries such as Canada and Australia have well-developed public and private or separate systems that operate in the same communities. If educational voucher and tuition tax credit plans become popular, the disturbed, reactive environment could become the predominant atmosphere for school organizations in the United States.

Turbulent fields are environments characterized by complexity, rapid change and clustering. In this type of environment, conditions are so complex that it is difficult to understand the combination of forces that create the constant change. Multiple factors experience dramatic change and the changes are linked. The turbulent field can have overwhelmingly negative consequences for the organization; in fact, the environment may change so drastically that the survival of the organization is threatened. A distinctive feature of the turbulent field is the interdependence among environmental factors. By shifting together and influencing each other, the effects are magnified. True turbulent fields are rare, but when they occur, planning is of little value because the changes are so dramatic and rapid. Individual organizations cannot adapt successfully through their own actions. Rather, survival depends on the emergence of values that have overriding significance for all members of the field. Social values are coping mechanisms that make it possible to deal with persisting areas of relevant uncertainty. Good illustrations of the turbulent field are difficult to formulate because the environment does not sit still long enough for examination.[18] However, the volatility of the computer industry during the last decade might approximate the uncertainty depicted by the turbulent field environment.

Shirley Terreberry argued that the four types of environments described by Emery and Trist are stages in an evolutionary chain.[19]. Extrapolating from Terreberry's work produces the prediction that organizational environments are becoming increasingly turbulent. In today's society placid-randomized environments are probably quite rare. Schools are becoming more and more interconnected with and affected by other organizations, such as state departments of education, legislatures, universities and businesses.

[. . .]

In sum, the central characteristics of the information–uncertainty approach are three-fold. First, the focus is on the decision makers' perceptions of their environments rather than on the actual characteristics. Secondly, the fundamental hypothesis is that perceived environmental uncertainty affects the degree of flexibility and bureaucratic nature of organizations. Thirdly, the research approach is based on the subjective perceptions of environmental factors by organizational members.[20]

Resource dependency perspective

In contrast to the information perspective that treats environment as the flow of information, resource dependency theory views environment in terms of relative scarcity of resources, and neglects the processes by which information about the environment is gained by the decision makers. Resources are critical in this perspective. Four general types of environmental resources are typically identified – fiscal, personnel (e.g. students, teachers, administrators, school volunteers, and board members), information and knowledge, and products and services (e.g. instructional materials and test scoring services).[21]

Dependence is the other important concept of the perspective.[22] For educational settings, dependence of a school organization on another organization is directly proportional to the school organization's motivational investment in the resources controlled by a second organization, and inversely proportional to the availability of these resources from other organizations. That is, if the school organization cannot accomplish its goals without the resources controlled by the other organization and is unable to secure them elsewhere, the school organization becomes dependent on the second organization. Conversely, as resources are supplied, the other organization gains power over the school organization. It follows that the greater the resource dependence, the more the organizations will communicate with each other.[23] Notice that dependence is an attribute of the relationship between the organizations and not an attribute of the individual organization in isolation.

A recent set of events illustrates the dependence concept. During the past decade, as fiscal resources from local property taxes and federal grants declined, school districts had an increased motivational investment in securing additional appropriations from state legislatures. As greater percentages of their budgets were supplied by the state, the dependence of school districts on state governments grew dramatically. In a parallel fashion, the power of the state over local school districts expanded; when the reform movement of the mid-1980s began, state legislatures and offices of education were able to dictate educational reforms to school districts.

The fundamental assumption of resource dependency theory is that organizations are unable internally to generate all the resources and functions to maintain themselves.[24] Resources must come from the environment. As a consequence, organizations must enter into exchanges with environmental elements that can supply the needed resources. In exchange for resources, the external groups or organizations may not only consume the organization's outputs but demand certain actions from the organization. For example, individuals who have been educated and trained in the schools contribute their efforts to society, and society demands that schools offer particular types of training.

The fact that all organizations are dependent on their environments makes external control of organizational behavior possible and constraint inevitable. If they are not responsive to the demands of their environments, organizations cannot thrive. But demands often conflict; thus, organizations cannot thrive by simply responding completely to every environmental demand. The challenge for school decision makers is to determine the extent to which the school organization can and must respond to various environmental demands.

An organization's attempts to satisfy the demands of a given group are a function of its dependence on that group relative to other groups and the extent to which the demands of one group conflict with the demands of another. Three factors are critical in determining the dependence of one organization on another. First, the importance of the resource to the organization's continued operation and survival affects the level of dependency. Schools cannot exist without students, but they probably can survive without IBM and Apple computers. Secondly, organizational dependence is mediated by the amount of discretion the other organization has over the allocation and use of the resource. Legislatures hold immense power over schools because they have the discretion to make rules and appropriate the funds for specific educational programs. Finally, dependence is influenced by the number of alternatives or extent of control that the other organization has over the resource. In other words, the dependence of one organization on the other derives from the concentration of resource control. For example, school district dependence on the federal government lessened during the early 1980s because the reduction of federal funding was replaced by funds from local and state sources.

Organizations strive to avoid becoming dependent on others or to make others dependent on them. Therefore, the resource dependence model also portrays organizations as active and capable of changing and responsive to their environments. Administrators manage their environments as well as their organizations; in fact, Pfeffer maintains that managing the environment may be more important than managing the organization.[25] Members of the organization make active, planned and conscious responses to environmental contingencies. Organizations attempt to absorb uncertainty and interdependence either completely, as through merger or consolidation, or partially, as through co-optation or the movement of personnel among organizations. Attempts are made to stabilize relations with other organizations, using tactics ranging from tacit collusion to legal contracts. Educational organizations, for example, establish external advisory groups comprised of leading individuals from related organizations or publics to stabilize relationships with other important parties.

In a study based on resource dependency theory, Michael Aiken and Jerald Hage hypothesized that, as interdependence is established between organizations, problems of internal coordination and control increase.[26] Their findings indicate that organizations with more joint programs, and thus a higher degree of dependence on the environment, are more complex themselves, have somewhat less centralized decision-making processes, are more innovative, have greater frequency of internal communication, and tend to be less formalized than organizations with fewer joint programs. Support for the work of Aiken and Hage is provided by the findings of Mindlin and Aldrich[27] that the higher the dependence on other organizations, the lower the formalization and standardization of organizational structure.

In sum, three generalizations capture the essence of resource dependency theory.[28] First, as organizations become increasingly dependent on their environments for securing resources, they require and tend to exhibit a more flexible and adaptive structure, usually associated with less formal and standardized procedures and more decentralized decision making. Secondly, dependence on external elements for resources can lead to inter-organizational relationships such as joint programs and co-optation. Thirdly, research based on this perspective uses archival, observational and other 'objective' methods to gather data.[29]

Toward a synthesis of the two perspectives

An attempt to integrate the information and resource dependency perspectives has been made by Aldrich and Mindlin.[30] They note that discussions of uncertainty and dependence imply that the concepts vary independently of each other. For example, the information perspective maintains that instability and complexity of the environment, as perceived by decision makers, create uncertainty with which the organization must deal. Coping with uncertainty forces the organization to employ less formal and more decentralized decision-making processes. In contrast, the resource dependence holds that similar structural arrangements are necessary when, in the process of obtaining valuable resources, organizations become dependent on other organizations.

The perspectives can be joined in at least two ways. First, the probable joint impact of uncertainty and dependence can be considered. Aldrich and Mindlin argue that an interactive effect exists for uncertainty of information from the environment and dependence on the environment for securing scarce resources. They reason that the effects of either dependence or uncertainty will be felt most strongly when the other factor is also present. Secondly, the perspectives can be integrated through the study of decision makers' perceptions of the environment. While the information perspective immediately directs attention to the role of perception, perceptions of resource dependence by decision makers also clearly play a large part in determining their reactions to the environment.

Conceptual derivations and applications

Because environmental uncertainty and resource dependence threaten organization autonomy and effectiveness, administrators often try to minimize external effects on internal school operations. This strategic response raises questions about the extent to which school organizations control, or even create, their own environments.[31] Within limits, school organizations have the ability to define or enact their own environments.[32] Attempts to reduce uncertainty and dependence can be grouped as internal and inter-organizational coping strategies. Both sets of strategies are designed to protect key processes from environmental influences.

Internal coping strategies

Buffering, planning and forecasting. Organizations try to isolate their technical cores (e.g. instructional activities in schools) from external influences.[33] This strategy of isolation is based on the assumption that efficiency can be maximized only when the technical core is not disturbed by external uncertainties. A process for providing the insulation is to surround instructional activities with buffers that absorb uncertainty from the environment. Therefore, specific departments and roles are created in school organizations to deal with and absorb uncertainty and dependence from a variety of environmental elements. Purchasing, planning, personnel, curriculum and facilities departments are created to buffer teachers from factors in the school's environment. These departments transfer materials, services, information, money and other resources between the environment and school district. In addition, a primary role of the principal consists of dealing with parental complaints about teachers. The goal of buffering is to make the technical core as nearly a closed system as possible and, thereby, enhance efficiency.[34]

In unstable environments and high levels of dependency, buffering strategies probably will not adequately protect the instructional program from external influences. Under conditions of high uncertainty and dependence, school organizations can attempt to control environmental fluctuations by the more aggressive strategies of planning and forecasting. These strategies involve anticipating environmental changes and taking actions to soften their adverse effects. Under these circumstances, a separate planning department is frequently established. In unstable, complex and dependent situations, planners must identify the important environmental elements, and analyze potential actions and counteractions by other organizations. Planning must be extensive and forecast a variety of scenarios. As conditions continue to change, the plans must be updated.

Adjusting internal operations. Work based on environmental typologies and on innovation and change suggest a contingency approach to organizational design. The way an organization should be designed depends in part on its environment. In other words, no one best way exists to organize schools. Rather, the most effective school structure is one that adjusts to the dimensions of its environment. Several contingency approaches are useful.

The first researchers to indicate that different types of organizational structure might be effective in different situations were Tom Burns and G. M. Stalker.[35] In an early study of 20 English industrial firms, Burns and Stalker demonstrated the relationship between external environment and internal administrative arrangements. Using interviews with managers and their own observations, they found that the type of structure that existed in rapidly changing and dynamic environments was significantly different from the type that existed in stable environments. When the external environment was stable, the internal organization was 'mechanistic', i.e. characterized by formal rules and centralized decision making. Relying heavily on programmed behaviors, mechanistic organizations performed routine tasks effectively and efficiently, but responded relatively slowly to unfamiliar events. In highly unstable environments, the internal organization was 'organic', i.e. informal, flexible and adaptive. The emphasis was on informal agreements about rules, decentralized decision making, collegial relations, open communication and influence based on expertise. Burns and Stalker did not conclude that the mechanistic model was inferior to the organic model, but rather, that the most effective structure is one that adjusts to the requirements of the environment – a mechanistic design in a stable environment, and an organic form in an unstable environment.

[. . .]

According to resource dependency theory, the environment does not impose strict requirements for survival. Therefore, a wide range of possible actions and organizational structures are possible; hence, criteria guiding decisions and determining structures become both important and problematic. Internal power differences are important because no single optimal structure or set of actions aligns the organization with its environment. Instead, a range of choices or strategies of alignment is available. The influence of a variety of internal stakeholders may determine, in interaction with the demands of external constituencies, the response of the organization. Resource dependence theory highlights the importance of environmental factors in promoting and restraining organizational decisions and actions, yet at the same time leaves room for the operation of strategic choice on the part of organizational members as they maneuver through known and unknown contexts. In other words, the resource dependence model posits that although environmental influences are important, environmental constraints do not reduce the feasible set of structures to only one form. Rather, a variety of internal structures and actions are consistent with the survival of the organization, which means that although the organization may have the goal of survival, survival does not imply only a single or very limited set of structural forms.[36]

As a note of caution in applying the findings from contingency research, structural and process variations occur across schools as a result of active alternative generation and search procedures to adapt and change the environment. In fact, Boyd argues that schools are neither 'mirror images' of the communities they serve nor are they completely insulated bastions dominated by unresponsive and self-serving professional educators.[37] To a considerable extent, school organizations can shape their environments to fit their capabilities.

Spanning organizational boundaries. Creating internal roles that span organizational boundaries to link the school district with elements in the external environment is also an important strategy for coping with uncertainty and dependence. Two classes of functions are typically performed by boundary-spanning roles: to detect information about changes in the external environment and to represent the organization to the environment.

For the detection function, boundary roles concentrate on the transfer of information between the environment and school district. Boundary personnel scan and monitor events in the environment that can create abrupt changes and long-term trends, and communicate the information to decision makers.[38] By identifying new technological developments, curricular innovations, regulations and funding patterns, boundary personnel provide data which enable the school district to make plans and adjust programs. In contrast to buffering personnel, boundary spanners act to keep the school organization an open system in harmony with the environment. A number of individuals in schools, e.g. superintendents and principals, play both buffering and boundary-spanning roles.

For the representation purpose, boundary-spanning personnel send information into the environment from the organization. The idea is to influence other people's perceptions of the organization. School districts often have offices of public information whose express purpose is to communicate information to significant stakeholders. Other district offices also can serve this function. For example, community and adult education programs, which primarily attract taxpaying patrons, can exemplify the quality of instruction that is available to the district's students. Business and legal departments can inform legislators about the school district's needs or views on political matters. Similarly, the boards of education and school advisory committees link the school organization to important constituencies in the environment in a highly visible way where they will feel their interests are being represented. Thus, women, minority-group members and students are appointed in increasing numbers to a variety of advisory committees.[39] Managing the school's image can reduce uncertainty and dependence on the various elements in the environment.

Inter-organizational coping strategies

Thus far we have described ways in which school organizations can adapt internally to the external environment. Schools also reach out and change their environments. Two types of strategies are used to manage the external environment: establish favorable linkages with key environmental elements and shape the environmental elements. A point to be remembered about attempts to control the environment is that it, too, has some organized character and the ability to fight back.[40]

Establishing favorable linkages. In business organizations a favorite mechanism to reduce competition and dependence is the merger. If a source of raw material is uncertain, buying the supplier removes the dependence on the external element. Although educational organizations cannot rely on mergers, they can enter into joint ventures with other organizations. School districts contract with the private foundations, universities, and federal and state governments to share the risks and costs associated with large-scale innovations and research projects. Current examples of joint ventures include Headstart, Follow Through, Individually Guided Education, special education programs and vocational education. David M. Boje and David A. Whetten found that, from a variety of organizational linkage strategies, the number of joint ventures was the best predictor of organizational influence on the environment.[41]

Co-optation represents another strategy of developing favorable linkages. Co-opting means bringing leaders from important elements in the environment or the elements themselves into the policy structure of the school organization. Co-optation occurs when influential citizens are appointed to boards of education or to advisory committees. The evidence, however, is mixed for increasing the influence of organizations through advisory councils. The research by Pfeffer[42] was supportive, although the findings of Boje and Whetten[43] were not. Another typical example of co-optation is the hiring of militant teachers or other activists to administrative positions. In these roles the co-opted individuals have an interest in the school and are introduced to the needs of the district. As a result they are more likely to include the district's interests in their decision making and less likely to be critical of the decision in which they participated.

Shaping environmental elements. Politicking is a primary method of shaping environmental elements for school districts. Political activity includes techniques to influence government legislation and regulation. School district officials and paid lobbyists express their views to members of state and federal legislators and other governmental officials. Political strategy can be used to erect barriers against unwanted influences and to establish rules favorable to existing schools and their policies. For example, public schools have engaged in extensive efforts to block state and federal support to private schools. Intense lobbying campaigns have been made against proposals concerning tuition tax credits and educational vouchers.

A related strategy to shape the external environment is forming educational associations that usually have both professional and political missions. Stephen P. Robbins termed this tactic 'third party soliciting'.[44] A significant portion of the work to influence the environment for education is accomplished jointly with other organizations that have similar interests [. . .] By pooling resources, individual educators or educational organizations can afford to pay people to carry out activities such as lobbying legislators, influencing new regulations, promoting educational programs, and presenting public relations campaigns. [. . .]

The overall implication for practice is that school organizations do not have to be simple passive instruments of the external environment. Both internal and external coping strategies can be used to buffer environmental influences and actually to change the demands. Structures, programs, and processes can be developed by educational administrators to manage the environments of their school organizations.

Summary

The emergence of open-systems theory during the past two decades has highlighted the importance of the external environment on internal school structures and processes. Although it does not have a firm definition, environment can be understood by its most salient dimensions. In this regard, a useful distinction is between broad factors, which are general trends that can *potentially* affect school operations, and specific factors, which are elements or conditions that have immediate and direct effects on schools. Moreover, three general characteristics – uncertainty, clustering and scarcity – are useful in the analysis of environments of schools.

Two perspectives of the environment have been developed, using the three general factors. The information perspective assumes that the environment is a source of information to be used by organizational decision makers. An important tenet of this approach is that perception is the intervening link between the school's environment and actions taken by decision makers. Research supports the fundamental hypothesis that perceived environmental uncertainty affects the degree of flexibility and bureaucratic configuration of organizations. In contrast, the resource dependency approach assumes that organizations cannot generate internally the needed resources and that resources must come from the environment. As a result, this perspective treats the environment as the degree of scarcity available to maintain stability and growth. School organizations, then, must enter into exchanges with environmental elements that supply the needed resources and can use the products and services of the school. The two perspectives can be joined in two ways. Uncertainty of information and resource dependence interact to enhance the other's effect, and both rely on the environmental perceptions of decision makers.

Because environmental uncertainty and resource dependence threaten organizational autonomy and effectiveness, administrators often try to minimize external effects on the internal school operations. Their responses can be classified as either internal or inter-organizational coping strategies. Internal coping strategies include buffering the technical core, planning and forecasting, adjusting internal operations based on contingency theory, and spanning organizational boundaries. Inter-organization coping strategies include establishing favorable linkages with important external constituencies and shaping environmental elements through political actions. By using the coping strategies, school administrators can to some degree reduce the environmental uncertainty and dependence of their school organizations.

Notes

1 William L. Boyd and Robert L. Crowson, 'The Changing Conception and Practice of Public School Administration,' *Review of Research in Education*, **9** (1981), 311–73.
2 James L. Bowditch and Anthony F. Buono, *A Primer on Organizational Behavior* (New York: Wiley, 1985), p. 158.
3 Ibid., p. 159.
4 Two other perspectives of organizational environments, population ecology and institutionalization, will not be considered. Sources presenting the population approach include the following: Glenn R. Carroll, 'Organizational Ecology,' *Annual Review of Sociology*, **10** (1984), 71–93; Michael T. Hannan and John Freeman, 'Structural Inertia and Organizational Change,' *American Sociological Review*, **49** (1984), 149–64; Michael T. Hannan and John Freeman, 'The Population Ecology of Organizations,' *American Journal of Sociology*, **82** (1977), 929–64; and Bill McKelvey, *Organizational Systematics: Taxonomy, Evolution, Classification* (Berkeley, Calif.: University of California Press, 1982). Sources presenting the institutionalization perspective include the following: Paul DiMaggio and Walter Powell, 'The Iron Cage Revisited: Institutional Isomorphism and Collective Rationality in Organizational Fields,' *American Sociological Review*, **48** (1983), 147–60; John Meyer and Brian Rowan, 'Institutionalized Organizations: Formal Structure as Myth and Ceremony,' *American Journal of Sociology*, **83** (1977), 340–63; Brian Rowan, 'Organizational Structure and the Institutional Environment: The Case of Public Schools,' *Administrative Science Quarterly*, **27** (1982), 259–79; Pamela S. Tolbert, 'Institutional Environments and Resource Dependence: Sources of Administrative Structure in Institutions of Higher Education,' *Administrative Science Quarterly*, **30** (1985), 1–13; and Lynne Zucker, 'Organizations as Institutions,' *Research in the Sociology of Organizations*, **2** (1983), 1–47.
5 Lee G. Bolman and Terrence E. Deal, *Modern Approaches to Understanding and Managing Organizations* (San Francisco: Jossey-Bass, 1984), p. 44.
6 Richard L. Daft, *Organization Theory and Design* (St. Paul: West, 1983), p. 42.
7 W. Richard Scott, *Organizations: Rational, Natural, and Open Systems* (Englewood Cliffs, N.J.: Prentice-Hall, 1981), p. 165.
8 Gerald Zaltman, Robert Duncan and Jonny Holbek, *Innovations and Organizations* (New York: Wiley, 1973), p. 114.
9 Ibid.
10 The discussion of general and specific environments relies on the ideas presented by Bowditch and Buono, *op. cit.*, pp. 159–60.
11 Ray Jurkovich, 'A Core Typology of Organizational Environments,' *Administrative Science Quarterly*, **19** (1974), 380–94.
12 Ibid., p. 382.
13 James D. Thompson, *Organizations in Action* (New York: McGraw-Hill, 1967), pp. 10–13.
14 Daniel Katz and Robert L. Kahn, *The Social Psychology of Organizations*, 2nd ed. (New York: Wiley, 1978), pp. 126–8.
15 Ibid.
16 Howard Aldrich and Sergio Mindlin, 'Uncertainty and Dependence: Two Perspectives on Environment,' in Lucien Karpik (ed.), *Organization and Environment: Theory, Issues and Reality* (Beverly Hills, Calif.: Sage, 1978), pp. 149–70.

17 Fred E. Emery and Eric L. Trist, 'The Causal Texture of Organization Environments,' *Human Relations*, **18** (1965), 21–32. The presentation of the typology relies on the works of Emery and Trist, ibid.; and Daft, *op. cit.*, pp. 52–3.

18 Bowditch and Buono, *op. cit.*, p. 164.

19 Shirley Terreberry, 'The Evolution of Organizational Environments,' *Administrative Science Quarterly*, **12** (1968), 590–613.

20 An excellent evaluation is made of the most frequently used perceptual measures of uncertainty by H. Kirk Downey, Don Hellriegel and John W. Slocum, Jr., 'Environmental Uncertainty: The Construct and Its Application,' *Administrative Science Quarterly*, **20** (1975), 613–29.

21 Howard Aldrich, 'An Organization-Environment Perspective on Cooperation and Conflict between Organizations in the Manpower Training System,' in Amant R. Negandi (ed.), *Conflict and Power in Complex Organizations* (Kent, OH: Center for Business and Economic Research, Kent State University, 1972), pp. 11–37; and J. Kenneth Benson, 'The Interorganizational Network as a Political Economy,' *Administrative Science Quarterly*, **20** (1975), 229–49.

22 Aldrich and Mindlin, *op. cit.*, pp. 156–7, trace the development of the dependency concept through the following works: Richard Emerson, 'Power-Dependence Relations,' *American Sociological Review*, **27** (1962), 31–41; Peter Blau, *Exchange and Power in Social Life* (New York: Wiley, 1964); David Jacobs, 'Dependency and Vulnerability: An Exchange Approach to the Control of Organizations,' *Administrative Science Quarterly*, **19** (1974), 45–59; and Sergio E. Mindlin and Howard Aldrich, 'Interorganizational Dependence: A Review of the Concept and a Re-examination of the Findings of the Aston Group,' *Administrative Science Quarterly*, **20** (1975), 382–92.

23 Andrew H. Van De Ven and Diane L. Ferry, *Measuring and Assessing Organizations* (New York: Wiley, 1980), p. 311.

24 The primary proponent of resource dependency theory probably has been Jeffrey Pfeffer. References to his work include the following: Jeffrey Pfeffer, *Organizations and Organization Theory* (Boston: Pitman, 1982), pp. 192–207; Jeffrey Pfeffer, *Power in Organizations* (Boston: Pitman, 1981), 99–115; Jeffrey Pfeffer, 'Size and Composition of Corporate Boards of Directors: The Organization and Its Environment,' *Administrative Science Quarterly*, **17** (1972), 218–28; Jeffrey Pfeffer and Gerald Salancik, *The External Control of Organizations: A Resource Dependence Perspective* (New York: Harper and Row, 1978); Jeffrey Pfeffer and Huseyin Leblebici, 'The Effect of Competition on Some Dimensions of Organizational Structure,' *Social Forces*, **52** (1973), 268–79; and Howard W. Aldrich and Jeffrey Pfeffer, 'Environments of Organizations,' *Annual Review of Sociology*, **2** (1976), 79–105. The present discussion of resource dependency theory draws heavily from these sources.

25 Jeffrey Pfeffer, 'Beyond Management and the Worker: The Institutional Function of Management,' *Academy of Management Review*, **1** (1976), 36–46.

26 Michael Aiken and Jerald Hage, 'Organizational Interdependence and Intra-Organizational Structure,' *American Sociological Review*, **33** (1968), 912–30.

27 Mindlin and Aldrich, *op. cit.*

28 Aldrich and Mindlin, *op. cit.*, p. 161.

29 An excellent example of using the 'objective' types of measurement in dependency theory is found in the study by Derek D. Pugh, D. J. Hickson, C. R. Hinings and C. Turner, 'The Context of Organizational Structure,' *Administrative Science Quarterly*, **14** (1969), 91–114.

30 Aldrich and Mindlin, *op. cit.*, p. 157.
31 Bowditch and Buono, *op. cit.*, p. 165.
32 Karl E. Weick, *The Social Psychology of Organizing* (Reading, Mass.: Addison-Wesley, 1969).
33 Thompson, *op. cit.*, pp. 19–24, discusses buffering, smoothing, forecasting and rationing as internal coping mechanisms. For educational organizations, buffering, planning and forecasting appear to be widely applicable and, therefore, the present discussion focuses on these strategies.
34 Daft, *op. cit.*, p. 56.
35 Tom Burns and G. M. Stalker, *The Management of Innovation* (London: Tavistock, 1961).
36 Aldrich and Pfeffer, *op. cit.*, pp. 83–4.
37 William L. Boyd, 'The Public, the Professional, and Educational Policy Making: Who Governs?', *Teachers College Record*, **77** (1976), 539–77
38 Daft, *op. cit.*, pp. 56–8.
39 Howard Aldrich and Diane Herker, 'Boundary Spanning Roles and Organization Structure,' *Academy of Management Review*, **2** (1977), 217–30.
40 Katz and Kahn, *op. cit.*, p. 131.
41 David M. Boje and David A. Whetten, 'Effects of Organizational Strategies and Contextual Constraints on Centrality and Attributions of Influence in Inter-organizational Networks,' *Administrative Science Quarterly*, **26** (1981), 378–95.
42 Pfeffer, *op. cit.*, 1972.
43 Boje and Whetten, *op. cit.*
44 Stephen P. Robbins, *The Structure and Design of Organizations* (Englewood Cliffs, N.J.: Prentice-Hall, 1983), p. 163.

4

Marketing educational services

Lynton Gray

Schools and colleges have always marketed themselves. Until recently this has been done discretely, patchily and instinctively, with little formal organization, minimal expenditure, and even less reference to those canons of marketing which shape the marketing operations of industrial and commercial organizations. This is now changing rapidly. Further and higher education has been exhorted to market itself more professionally, and has responded with energy and enthusiasm to the challenge. The schools sectors now face similar challenges. This chapter looks first at some of these, and explores some of the initiatives, ideas and theories currently underpinning the marketing of educational services. It then goes on to suggest ways in which the education service might make use of principles and concepts underpinning the marketing of some commercial services, and the limitations of such adaptations from the private sectors. It concludes with some suggestions as to ways in which the education service might develop approaches to the marketing of educational services which derive from sound educational practice.

Marketing and the Education Reform Act 1988

Key words and phrases in the 1980s include 'responsiveness', 'a market-oriented approach', 'choice', 'customer satisfaction', 'parent power' and 'competition'. The notions of privatization, of greater competition and the operation of free market economics in the public sector, and of consumer control, have pervaded government policies and legislation throughout the 1980s, and have come together most strikingly in the 1988 Education Reform Act. Educational institutions are being urged to adopt approaches which emphasize the provision of educational services as a response to the needs and demands of a variety of clients (e.g. parents and employers) and customers (students). The debates of the last decade have not focused primarily upon the principles involved. The notion of the education service responding to the needs of students and their actual and potential employers has not seriously been challenged. The key controversies have not been about whether the education service should be responsive, but about the groups to which it ought to be most responsive, about how it should demonstrate its responsiveness, and about who might legitimately define the needs of the client groups. The view that the professionals within the education service are best placed to define these needs and appropriate responses to them is still strongly held. However, the 1988 Education Reform Act has dealt a major blow to those holding this viewpoint, shifting powers and responsibilities away from the professionals to central government and lay governing bodies. The Act establishes new ground rules for education in which effective marketing becomes an essential requirement for every educational organization.

The further and higher education sectors have been enjoined from a number of directions and for several years now to improve their marketing. The White Papers *Training for Jobs* (DES/DE, 1984) and *Higher Education: Meeting the Challenge* (DES, 1987), the Audit Commission (1985), the Manpower Services Commission (MSC), the Further Education Unit (FEU) and a wide range of industrial and commercial spokespersons have all in their different ways played the same song. The marketing messages to the further education sector have been backed by resources from the MSC (now the Training Agency), so that colleges and local authorities have received funding in order to improve their marketing, both in the form of grants to colleges to support the appointment of full-time marketing managers, and through substantial support to the Responsive College Programme, based at the Further Education Staff College. Other government support for the improvement of college marketing has come through the DES-funded PICKUP (Professional, Industrial and Commercial Updating) scheme and a host of short-term support schemes such as the College-Employer Links Project.

The results of this combination of instruction, exhortation and investment in the further education sector are clearly visible. The majority of colleges have now appointed an individual or group of people with responsibility for college marketing. Furthermore, whereas the first appointments were of relatively junior if enthusiastic members of staff, allocated 3–4 hours per week for the task of marketing their college's services, more recently more senior appointments, at the level of head of department or vice-principal have been made, with more realistic resource and time support. Furthermore, a growing number of local authorities are employing marketing officers with responsibility for marketing the post-schools services of the whole Authority (Megson, 1988).

Marketing is, therefore, now established as a necessary part of the management function in the post-school sectors. Colleges recognize that they are competing for a declining number of 16-year-olds, and competing not only with other colleges but with schools, private training organizations and, increasingly, industrial and commercial organizations which are responding to demographic decline by seeking to employ workers at the age of 16, before training. Higher and some further education institutions are also marketing their services overseas, in order to attract overseas students. The marketing strategies employed by colleges are becoming increasingly sophisticated, as they deploy a remarkably extensive range of promotional devices in order to sell their courses and enhance their images. The first textbooks and practical manuals assisting college marketing personnel have appeared (Davies and Scribbins, 1985; Baber and Megson, 1986; Keen and Greenall, 1987; Walker and Hooper, 1988). These draw both from practical educational marketing experience and from industrial and commercial marketing, applying and adapting the precepts used in private sector marketing and public relations to the marketing of educational services. There is still no British equivalent to Kotler and Fox's (1985) major American handbook on marketing for educational institutions.

The schools sectors have responded less rapidly to the need for marketing. The 1980 Education Act required them to provide information for parents, normally in the form of school brochures. The Act also increased competition through the introduction of the Assisted Places Scheme, removed restrictions upon the free movement of pupils across LEA boundaries, and attempted to restrict the circumstances under which pupils would be refused admission to schools (Brunt, 1987). The 1988 Education Reform Act goes much further than this, with the explicit intention of increasing competition in public sector education at every level. Physical capacity becomes in effect the only constraint upon the free movement by pupils to the school of their (or their parents') choice. The 'opting-out' clauses have made it more difficult for local authorities to manage the overall provision of school places. Grant-maintained schools will compete with LEA-maintained schools and private schools, in a less regulated market, for pupils whose total numbers will continue to decline in the secondary sector into the early 1990s. There is already massive over-provision nationally of the total numbers of places, and competition for 11-year-old students will intensify in the years ahead, as central government policies make it increasingly difficult for local authorities to manage this over-provision by school closures. Such competition is likely to be fuelled by the Act's 'local management of schools' clauses, which will enable schools to earmark resources to support the marketing function, albeit at the expense of other activities. The competitive climate has been reinforced by further government actions, including the establishment of city technology colleges, and the 1988 Local Government Act's requirements for compulsory competitive tendering.

Few schools have as yet developed marketing approaches as comprehensive or as sophisticated as those of colleges, polytechnics and universities.

School brochures are rarely as seductive as the better college publications. Promotional strategies such as the use of video and media advertising are found less frequently in the school sectors, although schools in the private sector are increasingly skilled in promoting themselves, individually and collectively through ISIS (the Independent Schools Information Service). A distinct marketing function, organized with personnel holding clearly defined marketing responsibilities, is not normally recognizable in schools. It is subsumed among the various management responsibilities of the head and senior management team. The 1988 Act is likely to heighten schools' recognition of the importance of marketing, and cause a growing number of schools to re-examine their marketing strategies and organization. The next sections explore some of the issues likely to be faced by schools and colleges as they undertake this re-examination.

The marketing of service industries

The basic principles of marketing derive from the marketing of industrial products such as cars and consumer durables. The basic textbooks (e.g. Kotler, 1986; Cameron *et al.*, 1988) emphasize these industrial and commercial examples, and posit a rational marketing sequence of activities, summarized in Fig. 4.1. Thus an organization identifies the need to market a new product, or improve the marketing of a product whose sales are declining or otherwise causing problems. It therefore undertakes a marketing audit, identifying distinctive market segments and their characteristics, and carries out forms of marketing research into the preferences and expectations of a

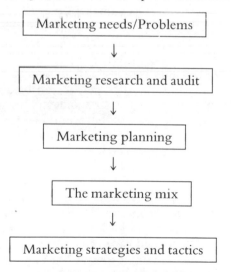

Figure 4.1 A basic marketing management model.

sample of those market segments, exploring marketing opportunities in existing and new markets. On the basis of the evidence from the audit and the marketing research a marketing plan is drawn up, which spells out selected target markets and predicted demand rates. Central to the plan is the notion of the 'marketing mix' of the '4 P's' – *product, place, price* and *promotion*. Each of these is considered in turn, in order to achieve an effective balance of marketing activities, through which the organization then implements the marketing plan by means of an agreed set of major strategies and detailed tactics. Davies and Scribbins (1985) demonstrate clearly the application of this approach to the marketing of further and higher education. Its value lies largely in the systematic nature of the approach, the emphasis given to the collection of evidence through research and audit, and the clear demonstration that marketing amounts to a lot more than selling, advertising and public relations.

Whereas this marketing model might be wholly appropriate for some manufacturing industries, its applicability both within the public sector and in service industries has been questioned (Cowell, 1984). To begin with, the model is structured around the concept of a 'product' – something tangible, with an identifiable manufacturing cost and a clearly marketable image. The success of the marketing function can, therefore, be measured in relation to the profitability of the manufacturing company and, more precisely, in terms of the numbers of items sold and the gap between the manufacturing cost and the sale price. A service industry does not sell a tangible product as such at all. A public sector organization is not measured in terms of profitability or 'mark-up'. Public sector service industries are heavily dependent upon the commitment and competence of employees, whose objectives may well be at odds with the employing organization's formal objectives. Educational organizations need, therefore, when seeking marketing analogies and models, to consider the distinctive characteristics both of service industries and of the public sector.

Service industries such as banking and tourism have some lessons for the education service, without necessarily prescribing the details of an appropriate marketing strategy. The tourist industry resembles education in that it offers unmeasurable 'dreams', which promise – or hint at – outcomes in terms of future well-being which cannot be guaranteed. The likely benefits of a number of GCSE grades or a 2nd class honours degree are at least as difficult to quantify as the consequences of a fortnight in Lanzarote. Similarly, while both services can describe in general terms the processes to be undertaken in order to achieve those outcomes, neither can offer many guarantees about those processes, whether they be uncrowded beaches, congenial company or exciting classes. Both tourism and education face a common service industry problem of lost sales. The unsold car can be stored in a showroom and its price manipulated until a purchaser is found. The unsold seat, whether in an aircraft or a classroom, is lost forever, so that service industries have the double-edged problem of an intangible product which, none the less, if not taken up, represents a very real loss of income to the industry. Travel agencies and airlines have a wide range of ploys to overcome these problems and to minimize such lost income. Education, despite the Audit Commission's (1984) quantification of surplus seats in secondary schools at £230 per place per year, not only has yet to develop appropriate strategies, but is ambivalent as to whether it is indeed a problem at all. The notion that the smaller the class the better the educational quality is persistent and supported with some research evidence. The private sector of education takes advantage of this by manipulating fees so as to make a promotional feature of small classes – and charge accordingly. But for most pupils and students education in a small class is an unexpected and probably unsought quasi-benefit. The new funding arrangements of the 1988 Act will highlight lost income from empty seats. Many schools may then choose to market as aggressively as some tour operators in order to avoid this lost income. Advice given to those marketing tourism on publicizing spare capacity (e.g. Holloway and Plant, 1988) may be adaptable to the needs of education – another industry with a powerful seasonal pattern.

Another service industry with some possible lessons for the education service is banking. Like education it has been criticized for being insensitive to the needs of its customers, and the government has altered the regulations governing the industry's operation, encouraging new forms of competition from building societies, etc. The provision of financial services has become more flexible, with extended opening hours, greater investment in high-technology electronic systems, and massive advertising campaigns by all the major banks. Lessons for the education service include the increased responsiveness to customer preferences in the face of increased competition, and the development of forms of non-contact services (banking's equivalent to distance learning, with cash machines and electronic point-of-sale transactions). The banks also demonstrate very obvious market segmentation, with aggressive competition for the student market accompanied by gifts and other inducements, in contrast to the lower-key pursuit of the wealthier market segments with differential interest rates, a wide array of sophisticated financial services and status symbol gold cards.

Research into the marketing of service industries suggests that the traditional 'four P's' model is deficient. Cowell (1984) suggests three more P's – people, process management and physical evidence. Whereas the last two seem to be dredging unnecessarily to find further 'P's', the emphasis on people is a distinctive feature of service industries. Any service is dependent on the staff who deliver that service, to a degree not normally associated with the manufacture of products. The service to a very real extent *is* the people who deliver it. The marketing of tourism and banking both demonstrate this. Codes of conduct attempt to provide substitutes for the quality control mechanisms used on assembly lines. These specify both how employees in the industries should behave and how customers should be treated. The processes of customer contact are rationalized in both industries, both using computerized technology and simplifying contact for customers through automatic teller machines in banking, and through package arrangements in tourism. Where face-to-face contact between customers and employees is necessary, both industries invest heavily in training employees in appropriate patterns of behaviour and the relevant interpersonal skills. These are backed by distinctive staff reward structures in the form of exotic holidays and no- or low-interest loans. The relevance of such strategies to the relationships between educational organizations and their employees is considered in the next section.

Tourism and banking are private sector industries, whose marketing successes are measured eventually by the extent to which they are able to anticipate, stimulate, regulate and satisfy customer requirements profitably. Public sector organizations are not yet measured in terms of their profitability. They are now exhorted – and even required – to utilize the substitute of 'cost-effectiveness' in place of profitability. There is at present a considerable – and so far not obviously successful – search for some equivalent to profitability in terms of 'performance indicators' (e.g. CIPFA, 1988). A marketing perspective can assist this process, by developing and using measures of customer satisfaction. The Responsive College Programme has developed and piloted several relatively simple instruments for gauging levels of further education student and employer satisfaction (Responsive College Project, 1988). The 1986 (No. 2) Education Act already requires schools to hold annual parents' meetings – crude devices for assessing customer satisfaction – but these could fruitfully be complemented by relatively simple surveys of both parental and student satisfaction levels.

Marketing and personnel management in education

Marketing is an important management function, in education as elsewhere. It is closely related to the other key functions of an educational organization – personnel, curriculum and resource management. The next sections examine these relationships in more detail. A central concern is the exploration of ways in which the distinctive characteristics of education and its management might contribute to an indigenous approach to marketing. Such an approach would build upon the strengths and traditions of the education service, and would disarm critiques of marketing which accuse it of polluting education with alien commercial ideas and strategies incompatible with the fundamental objectives of an education service.

Robinson and Long (1988) advocate 'internal marketing' as a distinctive requirement for service industries in general and educational marketing in particular. This is defined as selling the job to employees before an organization can sell its services to customers. Applied to further education, Robinson and Long (1987) argue that 'Good Marketing Practice = Good Teaching Practice'. A major aspect of customer satisfaction relates to the quality of the teaching, but marketing is not only about customer satisfaction, and customer satisfaction relates to more than teaching. Educational marketing is also concerned with the anticipation and development of new services to new market segments, and particularly to those segments with traditionally low involvement in education. It is also concerned with enhancing the corporate image of the organization and of the service generically. A concern for customer satisfaction includes the encouragement and promotion of the view that educational provision is a matter not just of current consumption – a major part of user satisfaction – but is also an investment in the future.

A marketing perspective is one which encourages all staff in educational establishments to recognize that they individually have marketing responsibilities, which include promoting the organization's image, and monitoring and enhancing customer satisfaction. Part of these responsibilities should be to shape client and customer perceptions so that they recognize and respond not only to the quality of the teaching, but also to the likely benefits arising from learning experiences. These could be learner-controlled in the form of distance learning, independent study and co-operative learning. An effective marketing strategy is one which seeks to influence the social encounters at school or college, the relationships with non-teaching as well as teaching staff and the overall ambience of the institution, and which heightens the teaching and non-teaching staff awareness of their roles in marketing the school services from the office telephone and the caretaker's office as well as the classroom.

This requires investment in staff development and training. Overall, a major objective of any educational organization's marketing and staff development strategies should be to enhance the organization's responsiveness to its clients and potential clients. Marketing research needs to examine carefully the significant points of contact between clients and the employees in educational institutions. Initial contacts are frequently fraught with problems. Despite the efforts of many further education colleges their enrolment procedures still resemble the supposed mating routines of some large and rare mammals – occurring annually, with maximum inconvenience and minimal pleasure to both parties.

Contact with educational institutions by telephone, letter or face-to-face is still unlikely to be as welcoming as your high street travel agent. Educational institutions need to shed the images of hostile secretaries, truculent or ignorant telephone receptionists, and incomprehensible, jargon-ridden written materials. This can be achieved by investing in forms of staff training, whose starting point is awareness raising. Despite the impact of falling rolls throughout the education service, teachers and non-teaching staff all too often do not perceive students and pupils as customers, whose patronage is needed if they are to hold on to their jobs. This initial contact or 'front-of-house' training is an important aspect of any institution's marketing planning. It needs to be augmented by strategies for improving the physical environment in which customer contacts take place, and by a stronger emphasis upon the potential benefits for clients, in both spoken and written forms of information. Useful lessons can be drawn from the better primary schools, which, despite severe resource constraints, have made great strides in recent years in improving the appearance of the environment, and in treating parents and pupils in more welcoming ways, including effective involvement of parents in the educational process itself. Most observers agree that the quality of teaching and learning have in consequence also improved.

One controversial strategy for heightening staff responsiveness to their customers would be to reward staff for particular demonstrations of effective marketing. The culture of the education service would probably resist attempts to emulate hotels in identifying, rewarding and publicizing the 'employee of the month'. However, the greater financial freedom which most schools, colleges and higher education institutions will have under the 1988 Education Reform Act makes it possible for institutions to develop imaginative forms of public recognition for those marketing activities which contribute to organizational survival and prosperity – and such activities must surely include particularly successful teaching. The requirements for the implementation of appraisal schemes under the 1986 (No. 2) Education Act provide further opportunities for such appreciation of high-quality work. Customer satisfaction surveys could well contribute to that appraisal process, as could the marketing research technique of spending part of a day following a randomly selected pupil or a class through the school's curriculum offerings.

Marketing and curriculum management

Central to the marketing of any educational service is a concern for the nature and the quality of the curriculum. An educational marketing strategy must, therefore, both take account of the curriculum and attempt to influence it. Marketing research will identify new curriculum needs, and ways in which the current curriculum provision should be improved. It should also identify 'market segments' who could and should benefit from forms of educational provision not currently available to them. The record of the education service in providing access for traditionally disadvantaged groups is improving. The 1981 Education Act drew attention to students with special needs and provided a framework for the improvement of their educational provision. Government funding has supported experiments in providing access courses in further and higher education, e.g. for women in science and technology. However, the education service has often not sufficiently publicized such developments, to the detriment not only of the educational institution but also of potential customers who have remained ignorant of the opportunities available to them.

Teaching and learning processes are as important to education's customers as the curriculum content. Some institutions have specialized in distinctive choice opportunities for their students, such as the North-East London Polytechnic's emphasis on independent study, Oxford Polytechnic's modular curriculum and, most notably, the Open University's use of distance learning, which has been emulated throughout the world. The institutions mentioned have promoted the distinctive nature of their curricula as part of their marketing strategies. Schools and colleges could well benefit from a closer examination from a marketing perspective of the curriculum choices available to their students, including the teaching and learning processes they are expected to undertake. Thomas (1986) is just one of a number of critics of the limited choice of opportunities in secondary schools, contrasting the opportunities available in good primary schools. The standardization imposed by a National Curriculum needs to be countered by a stronger emphasis upon the quality of learning opportunities and the individualization of learning. This is encouraged by the proposed assessment procedures for the National Curriculum (Task Group on Assessment and Testing, 1988), with the identification of a sequence of 'levels' through which pupils progress in each 'profile component'. In an increasingly competitive environment schools and colleges will need to identify responses attractive to potential clients, which emphasize the quality of curriculum provision rather than any distinctive content. They need then to develop strategies for drawing clients' attention to this.

Marketing and resource management

The 'marketing mix' approach is a device for examining the deployment and redeployment of resources. It requires consideration of the relative investment in:

- promotional techniques, including publicity materials, media relations and advertising;
- the 'product' (or service) – the curriculum and teaching/learning strategies, and most importantly the benefits thus accrued;
- the environment in which the service is delivered (the 'place');
- the cost asked of participants taking up these educational services (the 'price') including the fees and other expenses, as well as the opportunity costs to students choosing to buy education rather than spend their time and money elsewhere; and
- people, including staff development, training, organization and motivation, as indicated in the previous section.

An educational marketing strategy should, therefore, carry a price tag. A marketing audit should identify current resource deployment, and research findings may well suggest ways in which the same resources might be deployed more effectively.

A distinctive feature of the marketing function in the public sector is the expectation that it will generate new resources – commonly in the form of direct involvement in fund-raising. Some education sectors are becoming particularly adept at this, investing considerable resources (including staff time) and reaping substantial returns. Gorman (1988) describes a range of such strategies for schools. Marketing posts in further and higher education commonly require the holders to work actively in acquiring the additional resources associated with industrial and commercial sponsorship, Training Agency and other governmental funding, as well as income-generating activities such as short courses and consultancies. The annual publication *Paying for Training* (Planning Exchange, 1988) is indispensable for those whose jobs in further and higher education depend upon their successes in raising such funds.

Organizing for marketing

A checklist of the major marketing tasks to be undertaken in most educational organizations would include:

- liaison with feeder institutions;
- organizing student recruitment;
- employer/industrial/commercial liaison;
- fund-raising and sponsorship;
- promoting, costing and organizing income-generating activities including lettings and short courses;
- media relations and public relations;
- preparation of brochures and other publicity materials;
- marketing research;
- preparing marketing plans;
- managing 'front-of-house' environment, reception and other customer contact; and
- organizing related staff development and training activities.

An institution may seek to concentrate these tasks in the job description of one individual 'marketing manager', to distribute them among a marketing team, or to expect all managers – or at least senior managers – to take on these responsibilities.

The organizational location of the marketing function in further and higher education organizations has been discussed by Scribbins and Davies (1988). They emphasize that the marketing function is a key aspect of management, and examine the disadvantages of the 'sub-management model', whereby relatively junior staff are given responsibility for an organization's marketing. They also point to an emergent 'general and lieutenants model', whereby the advantages of institutional collaboration are enhanced by the LEA-wide organization of marketing under an LEA marketing co-ordinator. Megson (1988) provides some practical demonstrations of this approach.

As indicated above, marketing is a resource-consuming function, whose activities impinge directly upon the personnel and curriculum management functions. It is feasible, therefore, to identify marketing as a distinctive and specialist responsibility for a senior member of the institution's management team. In a large institution, this individual may delegate some of the tasks listed above to colleagues with specialist functions for employer liaison and as public relations officers, etc. It is equally feasible, given the all-pervading nature of a marketing perspective, for all senior managers to be expected to take on marketing responsibilities. If the latter organizational model is adopted it is vital that all managers are not only aware of and in agreement with the marketing perspective underlying the institution's philosophy, but also have the necessary specialist marketing capabilities to be able to put that philosophy into practice successfully.

At the heart of the effective organization of educational marketing is the marketing plan, which is likely, as schools and colleges move towards more formalized planning, to form part of the broader institutional 'development plan' or 'corporate plan'. Most local authorities now expect their schools to prepare 'institutional development plans'. The Training Agency requires local authorities to prepare 'work-related non-advanced further education development plans' for their further education colleges. The marketing plan forms a part of this strategic planning process. Detailed guidelines for the planning processes and their incorporation within the broader corporate plan (e.g. Macdonald, 1984) generally posit a rational planning model, whose applicability in educational institutions has yet to be tested.

Central to the planning process is the identification, development and promotion of a distinctive and consistent positive image of the educational organization. Marketing devices such as the use of a 'logo', school uniform or high standards of out-of-school behaviour, all play their part in this. Careful public relations, including a well thought-out media relations strategy also play their part. Many private schools successfully project images which prove extremely attractive to the market segment being pursued. Heavy government expenditure on the image of the city technology colleges demonstrates what can be achieved with a lavish marketing budget. Most educational organizations are not so generously resourced, but imagination and effort can often overcome the resource constraints, even to the extent of competing directly with the siren enticements of the private sector and city technology colleges. Basic marketing principles are important here: identifying clearly the market segments, and projecting to them through the most appropriate media the messages that these segments are seeking to hear. Of course, the messages must be backed by action in the school or college to ensure that public relations promises are borne out by the realities of the customers' educational experiences. Once again this underlines that the marketing plans and strategies must be directed internally as much as externally – and the former so often requires much more hard work and creativity than the latter.

Conclusions

This chapter has argued that a marketing perspective needs to infuse all educational organizations, and involve all staff. The marketing function is a necessary element of the management of educational institutions. In keeping with the growing formalization of institutional planning, the organization of educational marketing might include the following characteristics:

1 The establishment of marketing objectives and an organizational framework for marketing.
2 The systematic collection of marketing information through marketing audit and research.
3 The development of a costed marketing plan, based upon the 'five P's', which forms part of the educational organization's corporate plan.
4 The implementation and evaluation of the strategies and tactics agreed in the plan.

This does no more than redirect a well-tried and long-established approach to the management of education. Underlying it is the fundamental belief that the education institution is there to provide a service, and to respond to the needs of its pupils/students and their parents. The myth that the professionals within the education service were uniquely qualified to identify and express those needs has been exploded. The 1988 Education Reform Act formalizes the myth's demolition. A more systematic approach to the marketing of educational provision is an inevitable response to demographic change and to government policies which increase competition in the public sector. This need not, however, require the wholesale imposition of alien business techniques and unsavoury salesmanship. Sound educational practice has long emphasized collegial responsiveness to student needs. A marketing perspective presents opportunities to listen all the more carefully to the views of students and parents, to respond effectively to criticisms, and to emphasize student choice in the face of the constraints imposed by the National Curriculum. A marketing perspective emphasizes the need for collegial approaches by teaching and non-teaching staff, whose involvement in and commitment to educational marketing will determine whether or not an educational institution succeeds – or even survives. A marketing perspective might even check the impulse towards destructive forms of inter-institutional competition, and encourage the identification of ways in which institutions might more effectively collaborate locally and regionally. Finally, the required marketing skills include the redirection of some basic teaching skills, involving effective communication through a variety of media, tailored to customers whose needs have been carefully and skilfully analysed. Good marketing practice amounts to sound educational practice spiced by the adaptation of approaches effective in the marketing of other services. Schools and colleges now need to integrate these practices as central features of institutional management.

References

Audit Commission (1984). *Obtaining Better Value in Education: Aspects of Non-teaching Costs in Secondary Schools*. London, HMSO.
Audit Commission (1985). *Obtaining Better Value from Further Education*. London, HMSO.
Baber, M. and Megson, C. (1986). *Taking Education Further: A Practical Guide to College Marketing Success*. Stratford-upon-Avon, MSE Publications.
Brunt, M. (1987). 'Marketing schools'. In *Primary School Management in Action*, ed. Ian Craig. London, Longman.
Cameron, M., Rushton, R. and Carson, D. (1988). *Marketing*. Harmondsworth, Penguin.
Chartered Institute of Public Finance and Accountancy (1988). *Performance Indicators for Schools*. London, CIPFA.
Cowell, D. (1984). *The Marketing of Services*. London, Heinemann.
Davies, P. and Scribbins, K. (1985). *Marketing Further and Higher Education*. London, Longmans for FEU and FESC.
Department of Education and Science (1987). *Higher Education: Meeting the Challenge*. Cm. 114. London, HMSO.
Department of Education and Science/Department of Employment (1984). *Training for Jobs*. Cmnd. 9135. London, HMSO.
Gorman, G. (1988). *Fund-raising for Schools*. London, Kogan Page.
Holloway, J. C. and Plant, R. V. (1988). *Marketing for Tourism*. London, Pitman.
Keen, C. and Greenall, J. (1987). *Public Relations Management in Colleges, Polytechnics and Universities*. Banbury, HEIST Publications.
Kotler, P. (1986). *The Principles of Marketing*, 3rd edn. Englewood Cliffs, N.J., Prentice-Hall.
Kotler, P. and Fox, A. (1985). *Strategic Marketing for Educational Institutions*. Englewood Cliffs, N.J., Prentice-Hall.
Macdonald, M. (1984). *Marketing Plans*. London, Heinemann.
Megson, C. (1988). 'The merits of marketing'. *Education*, **172**(16).
Planning Exchange (for DES PICKUP) (1988). *Paying for Training*. Glasgow, Planning Exchange.
Responsive College Programme (1988). *Newsletter* No. 3, February.
Robinson, A. and Long, G. (1987). 'Marketing further education: Products or people?'. *NATFHE Journal*, March.
Robinson, A. and Long, G. (1988). 'Substance v. trappings in non-advanced FE'. *Journal of Further and Higher Education*, **12**(1), Spring.
Scribbins, K. and Davies, P. (1988). 'Organising for marketing'. *Management in Education*, **2**(1), Spring.
Task Group on Assessment and Testing (1988). *Report of the Task Group on Assessment and Testing*. London, DES.

Thomas, H. (1986). 'Choice in the education market'. *Educational Management and Administration*, **14**(2), Summer.

Walker, J. and Hooper, R. (1988). *Going to Market*. Preston, Responsive College Programme.

Section II

Specific relationships

5

Parental choice and voice under the 1988 Education Reform Act*

Adam Westoby

Introduction

A key aim of the 1988 Education Reform Act (the ERA)[1]† is to give parents more power over the state school system. This chapter considers the ERA's dual strategy for 'parent-driven' improvement of schools, through both parents' choices between schools and parental involvement in schools' governance. As the ERA comes into force over the next few years, and as research on its effects gathers momentum, it will be reasonable to measure the Act's effects against this strategy.

The argument proceeds as follows. It sketches the ERA's main provisions for empowering parents as 'consumers' and recalls that empirical research on how parents choose between schools, and which parents actively do so, offers some, but only rather general, conclusions. Further, parents' relationships with schools as organizations go wider than their decisions to send their children there; and the ERA strategy includes elements aimed at strengthening parents' influence upon the schools their children do attend. The chapter introduces the problem of the interrelationships between (i) parents' behaviour in choosing *between* schools, (ii) influences exerted by parents *within* school organizations, and (iii) the ways in which school organizations will respond to the two preceding factors.

It then outlines the conceptual framework which has been developed by Hirschman and others for analysing such interrelationships. His concepts of 'exit' and 'voice' are briefly sketched, together with his argument that,

*This article originated as a discussion paper for a research project directed by Professor Ron Glatter at the Open University School of Education, examining the implementation of the 1988 Act (CHARGE – Challenge and Response in the Government of Education). I am grateful to the other members of CHARGE for comments, and to Ben Cosin, John Rose and David Zeldin.
†Superscript numerals refer to numbered notes at the end of this chapter.

especially for organizations (such as state-funded schools) which mainly compete on quality, more extensive 'exit' weakens the 'voice' that could help them modify their performance.

The chapter goes on to spell out some further possible implications for the ERA's impact on the school system. It considers the importance of uncertainty concerning educational processes and outcomes. It discusses outcome measures which may influence parents, and the significance of peer group effects. It points to the lack of a mechanism for forming grant-maintained schools from scratch, and ways in which demand may try to circumvent this. And it reviews some changes that may be expected in decision making and micro-politics within schools, and in the politics of Local Education Authorities (LEAs).

Much of this chapter refers to the future and is to that extent speculative; however, I hope its deductions are grounded in common sense. The main purpose is to highlight some key questions which research upon the ERA should address, and which practitioners involved in the implementation of the Act may want to bear in mind. More tentatively, it suggests a conceptual framework within which such questions may be examined.

The role of parental choice

Early comment on the ERA was preoccupied with problems of transition. But its strategic intentions are best envisaged in terms of what is expected to happen when the main provisions have taken effect.

Several key provisions can be seen as linked to parental choices, taking effect mainly through competition between schools.[2] At the most immediate level, the competition is for pupils. More open enrolment will prohibit LEAs from setting administrative ceilings to their schools' intakes, and will allow (or compel) popular schools to admit up to a 'standard number', intended to reflect their physical capacity. Schools which opt out from LEA control (grant-maintained schools) will be able to expand, and will be eligible for 100% grants from central government to support approved capital expenditure. The expectation is that these steps of 'deregulation' will cause popular schools to expand (and, perhaps, reinforce those characteristics that make them popular) and cause unpopular schools to contract, and respond by altering themselves so as to become more popular.

Competition will have a direct financial element, to give schools 'a clear incentive to attract and retain pupils' (DES Circular 7/88, paragraph 105). Under the local management of schools (LMS) provisions, control of budgets covering most current spending (including all staff salaries) will be delegated to governing bodies of all secondary and many primary schools, as will the hiring and firing of all staff. Of LEAs' 'aggregated schools budgets' (which they must allocate among schools under settled formulae) a minimum of 75% must be distributed in proportion to the schools' (age-weighted) numbers of pupils. Grant-maintained schools will receive current funding from central government on a wholly per capita basis. Thus parents, in opting to send their child to a school, also opt to provide the school with a definite, externally fixed, quantum of additional revenue. The links between pupil numbers and revenue are close enough to resemble a form of educational voucher scheme (see Thomas, 1988).[3]

There is a clear analogy with competition among firms supplying a similar product. But there are also important differences, and some of these are recognized and catered for in the strategy. Consumers (i.e. parents/ families) can only 'purchase' a fixed amount of state-funded education. Moreover, in the age-range of compulsory schooling they are *obliged* to purchase that amount. The only area of consumer freedom is the choice of supplier. State-funded schools are only allowed to make small and peripheral charges (for instrumental music tuition, for example), and *price* competition between schools is thus restricted to the fee-paying sector. Competition between state-funded schools turns largely on the quality (or, more precisely, qualities) of the product.

Quality in education is, however, extremely difficult to judge, especially for many parents. The strategy therefore incorporates elements aimed at:

- standardizing a central part of the product offered by competing suppliers (the national curriculum); and
- requiring suppliers to submit to external tests of the effectiveness with which they are supplying part of their product, and to publish the results of those tests (targets of attainment and assessment via nationally prescribed tests).

It seems reasonable to view these central elements of the ERA (more open enrolment, opting out, the national curriculum and pupil assessment) as connected within an internally coherent strategy grounded in parental choice – one consistent with the neo-liberal thinking that has informed many other areas of Conservative Government policy. Such a view can suggest areas to which the strategy itself would look to judge its success or otherwise.

Aims and outcomes

However, two points are worth noting. The strategy (like others for expanding consumer choice) is not necessarily to be judged directly from its effects. Critics of the strategy may regard it as condemned by outcomes which its supporters would accept or welcome. If, for example, in ethnically mixed urban areas, widespread and active parental choices led to schools becoming more ethnically distinctive, the main arguments over this would reflect fundamentally different evaluations of choice versus racial integration. Similar considerations apply to social mixing – a goal of many comprehensive systems. An example from one of the towns where Stillman and

Maychell studied parental choice illustrates this. The town contained two comprehensive secondary schools – a former (and ancient) grammar school, and a former secondary modern near a large council estate. The LEA had designed geographically eccentric catchment areas in an effort to achieve more similar social mixes in the two schools. None the less, many council estate parents excluded from the former secondary modern school's catchment area opted back to it, freeing places at the former grammar school for more middle-class parents. There was also a pronounced difference of criteria in choosing a school: among parents at the former grammar school, academic record was easily the most important factor, whereas for parents at the former secondary modern, discipline was most often cited (Stillman and Maychell, 1986, pp. 115–19). In such a situation one's view of manipulating catchment areas will depend on one's evaluation of choice versus social mixing.

The second point generalizes from the first. It is that the internal coherence of the ERA strategy for parental choice between schools does not (despite its incorporating standardized pupil assessment) *require* that it be possible to agree on cardinal or even ordinal comparisons of schools' 'quality'. Advocates of the ERA have often suggested that 'popular' does equal 'better'. But the strategy is also coherent as one for satisfying rather diversified consumer preferences, with schools providing different types of education. This interpretation of the strategy is consistent with central ingredients of current professional opinion in education, stressing the specificity of families and their needs. The supremacy of parental wishes is expressed, sometimes vividly, in political advocacy of the strategy. Thus Sir Rhodes Boyson, a former Conservative education minister, has indicated that he would be in favour of Trotskyist schools, 'provided that only the children of Trotskyist parents went'.[4]

In what follows I discuss matters mainly in terms of parental choice among schools regarded as orderable in quality. But whether schools compete by striving to maximize test scores, by differentiating the educational experiences they offer, and/or in other ways, what is essential to the coherence of the strategy is that they attempt to satisfy consumer preferences. At bottom, the image of parents as consumers implies that the strategy is to be judged not from what happens to education, but from what parents think of what happens to education. This has clearly irked many critics of the ERA, but the importance in educational rhetoric of the idea of 'partnership' between parents and schools has inhibited them from criticizing it directly.

How do parents choose?

The ERA strategy raises a host of empirical questions about parents' behaviour in choosing between schools. How many parents, and which parents, are sensitive to what differences between schools? Where will they get their information, and how will the perceptions on which they base their decisions be formed? How far and in what ways do older children influence the decisions made on their behalf? How are individual decisions affected by informal networks and by 'group' psychologies?

The literature on this offers rather few general findings. There are some broad similarities between the features of schools which parents cite as desirable: practical features such as geographical convenience, plus, among educational characteristics, traditional academic qualities and good discipline – these are generally held as more important for secondary schools. In situations where children are normally allocated to a local school, but parents can request a place elsewhere, a minority (often a small minority) do so; however, awareness of the possibility of choosing, and frequently some conscious comparison of alternative schools, often goes much wider. The 'destinations' of requests to go to a different school tend to be clustered on fewer schools than their 'origins', and the schools on which requests cluster are usually ones in middle-class areas thought to have good academic standards. Findings on the social class distribution of those parents who are 'active' in choice, by seeking a school beyond their local or normal one, differ. In Scotland (University of Glasgow, 1986) and among black urban Americans (Jarvis, 1986) active choosers appear to reflect the surrounding distributions of occupational or educational categories, whereas in France (Ballion, 1986), and according to a computer simulation based on British Family Expenditure Survey data (Ashworth *et al.*, 1988), they appear to be more strongly drawn from the middle classes.[5]

Schools' responses

Beyond questions about parents' behaviour arise further questions about schools' responses. The imminence of more open enrolment has heightened interest in how schools may project an attractive 'image'. But schools may also be expected to respond to shifts in their patterns of enrolment, and in the array of requests to switch to them and/or away from them, in more complex ways. They will in any case often have difficulty in assessing how far increases, falls or changes in composition in their enrolments are due to local competition, or other exogenous factors. Moreover, the changed general conditions of parental choice may also be expected to affect schools' functioning as organizations – and thus, in due course, their character, and thereby the future array of options across which future parental choices are made.

In fact, the ERA strategy for schooling does rest on a broader model than that sketched above – of parents as consumers, 'purchasing' from independent and competing suppliers. The strategy has a second 'prong', based on the recognition that, in becoming customers of a particular supplier, parents also enter (or at least gain the possibility of entering) into the organization whose customer they become, and can influence what it does.[6]

They can thus pursue the educational offerings they desire directly, as well as by choosing or switching between schools, and several aspects of the strategy aim at reinforcing their ability to do this. The 1986 Education (No. 2) Act increased both governors' powers and parents' representation on governing bodies, and requires governing bodies to give an annual, formal account of the discharge of their responsibilities to an open meeting of parents. The most important ERA provisions are those on LMS and opting out. Those on LMS transfer numerous LEA powers to governing bodies, including control of budgets for most current spending, and the appointment and dismissal of all staff. The opting out provisions can have two sorts of effect. In schools that *do* opt out, all LEA powers pass to the governing bodies; and in schools that have not opted out, LEAs are placed under greater pressure to have regard to parents' wishes, in exercising the powers they retain, by the possibility of the school's opting out (or of a significant campaign for opting out developing). The stipulation of a national curriculum does not directly expand parents' powers within schools, but it is likely to limit the scope of teachers' professional autonomy and perhaps lead to a shift of relative influence from experts to laity.

A more rounded view of the ERA strategy, therefore – from either supporters' or critics' points of view – would see it not as limited to increasing parents' influence over schools and education as pure consumers, but as combining this with measures to strengthen their position in schools as organizations. How far – quantitatively and qualitatively – 'internal' parental influence will gain greater purchase over schools' functioning remains an open and very important question. But assessments of the ERA strategy's effects, even if they are limited to assessing it on its own terms, ought to take account of both these elements, and look at the potential interactions between them. It is among these interactions that some of the most interesting problems arise.

'Exit' versus 'voice'

A classic discussion of interrelationships between individuals' involvements with organizations as consumers and as organizational participants is Hirschman's (1970) *Exit, Voice and Loyalty*. Hirschman's starting point was the observation that competitive pressures on organizations do not necessarily have the results expected in traditional economic theory. In particular, organizations which decline, in the sense that their performance falls relative to those of their competitors, will not necessarily respond – or even attempt to respond – to the situation in such a way that they recover their position.

Hirschman has provided a framework of considerable generality. His exposition of it draws on a wide variety of phenomena, and subsequent research has applied the core concepts to a good number of others, ranging from the consequences of residential relocation for local government (Orbell and Uno, 1972; Sharp, 1984) to the management of difficult love affairs (Rusbult *et al.*, 1986). (Hirschman, 1981a, 1981b contain his reflections on research stimulated by the original 'model'.) In this section I simply point to some features of the model which may be important in the institutional context of English and Welsh education, as modified by the ERA.

One of Hirschman's core arguments has to do with the trade-offs between two mutually exclusive forms of consumers' response to dissatisfaction with their present supplier. They may *exit*, switching to the preferred product of a rival supplier, or they may exercise *voice*, making complaints, suggestions or threats aimed at improving their present supplier's performance. From the point of view of the organization, *voice* is generally a more explicit, 'information-rich' guide to how it might improve its performance (in the sense of retaining and attracting customers) than is exit. Indeed Young (1976) has proposed broadening the economist's concept of 'market failure' to situations where exit is ineffective in stimulating management and restoring performance relative to other suppliers.

One reason why exit can be ineffective is that voice and exit may pull in opposite directions. Specifically, an increase in competition between rival suppliers, which results in an increasing flow of 'exiting' customers in search of preferred products, may have the effect of weakening voice, at least in the organizations that are declining. The effect may thus be, by weakening their recuperative mechanisms, to accelerate the decline that first began to cause exits. Making exit easier may well atrophy voice; voice may be loudest, and perhaps of greatest effect, when monopoly conditions prevail and customers are securely 'locked-in'.

Hirschman takes state education in the United States, with private schools competing with the state schools, as one of his main examples to develop this point, and to establish the sorts of cases where easier exit may most weaken the recuperative effects of voice. These cases are most likely to be found, he argues, when suppliers compete for customers most of all on quality, and relatively little on price. The reason is that where competition is mainly on quality, it is those who care most about quality who will be the first to exit if (relative) quality declines. Yet these are often the same ones who would be most articulate and energetic in applying voice if they stayed. Easier exit, therefore, may not just weaken voice numerically, it can also tend to remove the most audible and effective voices. The process in a school system has some resemblances to that of differentiation between residential areas. Those affluent enough to leave undesirable neighbourhoods and purchase houses in more desirable ones do so, and by taking with them both wealth and capacity for influence, increase the differences that caused them to move. Indeed, the two processes may have significant overlap, both in so far as schooling is a motive for moving, and in that property values may be increased by good schools nearby.

Hirschman's concept of 'exit' need not be limited to those who are already consumers, and whose decisions are therefore limited to whether or not to switch to another supplier. Many of his main points apply to consumers' decisions on which supplier to choose on first entering the market. And, translated into the context of English schools, they prompt a number of questions. The most general is: how will the (formal and informal) 'parties' to school government respond to changes in parental choice? In particular, will schools from which parents (on the whole) opt *away*, respond by changing, or attempting to change, so as to attract more parents? It is clearly an essential part of the ERA strategy that (on the whole) they should, but will this in fact happen? The question is all the more important because of the absence of mechanisms for forming new schools.

A study of the effects of 'placing requests' in Scotland (University of Glasgow, 1986) identified some effects of a net flow of requests away from a school, including a fall in staff morale where the flow was substantial (this was counterbalanced by an increase in morale in the smaller number of schools attracting the placing requests). Taken overall, however, outflows of placing requests did not lead to curricular changes, and a number of head-teachers specifically asserted that they should not do so, even if movements were substantial. In this setting, therefore, there was little positive evidence of parental choice triggering 'corrective' mechanisms within the schools. As research on the effects of the ERA gets under way, it will be important to focus not only on why some schools succeed, but on how others respond to processes of decline.

Information and uncertainty

Education, and many educational decisions, are typified by high levels of uncertainty and ignorance, both among parents and, to a lesser extent, among producers. High rates of innovation in educational methods are, among other things, symptomatic of this; it is also one of the main reasons why educational organizations have been described as 'loosely coupled' (Weick, 1976) or even 'organized anarchies' (Cohen *et al.*, 1972). How will uncertainty – about what constitutes good education, and how it may be accomplished – affect (a) parents' choices between schools and (b) their choices between exit and voice when they are dissatisfied with their current school?

The use of voice is almost always an uncertain business. What are the chances of my efforts (and those of others, which I can only guess at) bringing about the sorts of changes which I want? And to what extent, and on what sort of timescale?[7] Hirschman's (1970) initial analysis contrasted the 'certainty of exit' in consumer choice with the 'uncertainties of voice', and therefore regarded uncertainty as a discouragement to voice, and an encouragement to exit. However with schooling, exit (the alternative school, or more generally choice between schools) is most certainly not certain. Whatever one's criteria, it is notoriously difficult to make an assessment of a school from external (and usually brief) examination alone. Yet this – plus word-of-mouth – is the maximum that most parents have to go on. And it is even more difficult to assess in advance how far a school will be appropriate for a particular child. In contrast, most (actively) dissatisfied parents will know their present school as well as they are ever likely to know it. In the case of schooling, therefore, the advantage may not lie with exit (true exit, that is – switching a child from one school to another), but rather with voice (or staying). And from the point of view of improvement of the supply (school) system as a whole, high levels of uncertainty will tend to make voice more important relative to exit, both because voice (unlike exit) is 'information-rich', and because switching may contain a significant 'random' element, by consumers who are dissatisfied but who know little of the alternative to which they are switching (Hirschman, 1981b, pp. 219–22).

The ERA strategy bears directly on such problems. In the first place it seeks to provide parents with publically ascertainable, standardized bench-marks which they can use to compare different schools, reducing the uncertainty of choosing between them: the aggregated results of nationally prescribed tests. (How far the reduction of uncertainty is a distinct intention of the strategy is a slightly different point.) And, secondly, it requires LEAs to develop systems for monitoring the performance of their schools. One could argue about how far national test measures (or LEAs' broader perform-ance indicators) can give a useful reflection, for example, of school effective-ness. But there does seem to be a *prima facie* case for expecting their introduction to have at least two sorts of effects on parent behaviour:

1 For parents to become more 'active' in selecting (or switching) schools for their own children.
2 For test scores in particular, being public, quantitative and easily com-parable across schools, to increase the relative importance of academic attainment among the factors affecting parents' choice of schools.

Indeed, some critics of national tests have claimed that they will lead to substantial, destabilizing 'migrations' of children from school to school in quest of the best test scores, and the excellence they are presumed to denote. In effect, such critics predict that reducing the perceived uncertainties of exit will greatly increase its extent.

Performance measures, peer group effects and selectivity

Most professional educationalists are sceptical about average test scores as measures of a school's performance. In response to such criticisms, test measures may now be corrected by a factor or factors reflecting social deprivation among pupils' families. In addition, measures have been sug-gested which take direct account of educational input as well as output, such as 'educational value added'.

Yet it is far from certain that parents who are active and reflective in choice will opt for schools with the highest (socially corrected) test scores, or even the highest 'educational value added'. One important reason lies in the character of 'peer group' effects. Put simply, these express the fact that statistical studies of the educational achievements of individual pupils show substantial, independent effects of various distinct factors, including the character (or 'effectiveness') of the school, the individual pupil's *own* social background and initial educational level, and the social and educational characteristics of the 'peer group' with whom the individual child is educated (see e.g. Murnane, 1986b; Arnott and Rowse, 1987).

The strength of peer group effects is something that has been much debated in the literature – not less vehemently because it is central to one's view of the effects of selective versus mixed-ability or comprehensive schooling. However, what is, I think, less disputed is that many parents who make active educational choices believe that their child's peer group is important. They believe that their child will achieve more in so far as she or he is in the company of more able schoolmates, and will achieve less in so far as her class includes more children with behavioural problems or poor attentiveness. And parents who regard peer groups as important will not necessarily favour a school with high 'educational value added' if, for example, its large 'value added' only reflects the difference between very low input scores and average-to-poor output scores. Indeed, as far as test scores corrected for social deprivation are concerned, such parents may attach more weight to the correction factors than to the test scores themselves.

Only a minority of schools and LEAs in England and Wales now have explicit forms of selection by ability. But the variety and complexity of admissions arrangements, and the fact that schools themselves often play an important practical part in applying LEAs' admissions criteria to the individual applicants, means that considerable scope for informal discretion exists. The main beneficiaries of the situation are parents with better education, more contacts, and an ability to 'work the system', i.e. those whose children generally have an educational head start anyway.

The ERA does not change the legal framework for admissions, except by forcing 'open enrolment' on LEAs. But it may increase the pressures on popular schools to operate informal selection, for several reasons. First, heads and teachers, anxious about measures of their performance, may be tempted to admit abler pupils and those with better family support and exclude those with problems. Secondly, parents whose children are already in the school and who believe peer group effects to be important may be happy to see the intake enriched. Thirdly, if the changes in the way schools are resourced and managed make them more sensitive to income from charges, donations, PTA activities, etc., and/or more eager for direct parental help with their work, there will be incentives to admit parents who are more affluent and/or active.

Informal selection within a formally comprehensive system is often to some degree covert, and to that extent difficult to detect. But it is to be hoped that some of the research on the effects of the ERA will evolve designs able to investigate it.

No entry

Hirschman developed his ideas on voice and exit partly as a critique of the economics of competition, which he felt had inadequate conceptual means to consider what happened to firms (apart from those rapidly expiring) when they lost their competitiveness. In fact, as he pointed out, many firms (including some very large ones) do grow sick, then recover, and often go through such cycles several times; competition works only in part by extinguishing the inefficient, and thus opening niches for new firms.

But an important limitation of the ERA reforms is that opting out is not paralleled by any mechanism whereby *new* grant-maintained schools can come into existence, using central government funds to satisfy a perceived demand. This is in contrast with the Conservative Government's enthusiasm for small, new, dynamic firms, and so on; LEAs are to be left with their monopoly of opening new free schools. How far this proves a weakness of the strategy depends on schools' mechanisms for responding to adverse patterns of parental choice. Prior to the ERA some of the advocates of more open enrolment suggested that it would entail significant numbers of un-popular schools closing (Brown *et al.*, 1985), but in the event no mechanism for forming new schools was built in. (However, in December 1988, a campaign was launched, with Conservative backbench support, to allow private schools to opt *in* to being grant-maintained schools, while retaining control of their intakes.[8])

For our purposes, an interesting question is what mechanisms or processes may come into play to circumvent the restrictions on entry. Here also economic analogies suggest some possibilities. Entrepreneurs often prefer (because of high set-up costs) taking over ailing companies to starting up new ones. Some firms, like some schools, can go into decline for reasons specific to themselves. For example, although the general market they serve is buoyant, they may be badly managed, with a dysfunctional internal culture, and thus falter while their closest competitors are performing adequately (or at least better than they are). The number of consumers they attract falls, and so does their share price. As such a firm (school) declines, small shareholders will in many cases exit (sell their holdings/withdraw or withhold their children), and it is sensible of them to do so, as their small holdings give them little leverage, through voice, to change the way the organization is run.

However, such a process, if it goes far enough, will create a niche or opportunity. For example, it may produce a situation where the *potential* value of the firm (if its net assets were realized, or if more dynamic management took it in hand, or as part of a commercial reorganization) greatly exceeds its aggregate share value. These are typical 'takeover' situations. Entrepreneurs may try to cash in on such opportunities either through management (as 'company doctors'), or through speculative share purchases, or both.

Relatively unsuccessful schools present partly analogous opportunities. The main attempts to take advantage of them come through management – principally, I would guess, with appointments of heads or other senior staff.[9] But shareholders' (i.e. parents') initiatives are not unknown. According to dinner-party evidence, a few years ago a sizeable group of parents from one of the primary schools local to me (in the London Borough of Brent) made a collective decision to send their children on to the adjacent comprehensive, not because they regarded it as a good school (they did not), but rather with the intention of acting, as a group, to 'take over' its moribund PTA and 'overhaul' the school. However, they failed, and all but one of them have now exited, most of the children having been moved to schools outside the authority.

But the ERA may significantly alter the conditions for such attempts in future – by staff, parents, or coalitions between them – with opting out perhaps providing the main new incentive.

It is true that most of the incentives for parents are weaker than those for speculative shareholders – parents are obliged to consume the ailing company's products while they speculate in it, they can neither increase nor realize their shareholding, and aside from improvement in the product, their 'capital gain' is purely ethical. But in some ways parents' political capacities may be greater than shareholders'. Because they are less atomized than shareholders, and have more complex and emotionally charged interests in the organization, the scope for political leadership and ideological influence can be wider.

Schools' politics

Many of my observations so far can be drawn together in the simple prediction that, if the ERA's strategy for improving schools that parents are dissatisfied with is to work, it is not the actions of the parents who opt away from them that will produce changes (except very indirectly), but rather the behaviour of those – parents and others – who get and remain involved in them. And whether the second 'prong' of the ERA's strategy for parental power will be effective turns on how far parents prove able to wield sustained and constructive influence in school decision making and micro-politics.[10]

Some of the evidence suggests that their capacity to do this may be quite limited. Up to the very recent past most governing bodies have 'interfered' little in the curriculum, staffing and other substantial questions, and have generally rubber-stamped the head's decisions. PTAs and similar bodies, even where they are active, have no legal status or rights and frequently busy themselves mainly with fund-raising and social activities. The 1986 Act has increased the proportion of parent governors, but they remain a minority, and do not have representative status. As stated earlier, the 1986 Act also introduced annual, formal meetings at which governing bodies are required to give parents an account of the discharge of their responsibilities; however, in their first 2 years these meetings were seldom animated and often very poorly attended.

Apathy, however, may only reflect past impotence. Between 1988 and 1993 the ERA (and the 1986 Act) will transfer a series of very substantial legal and administrative powers from LEAs into the schools, most of them to the governing bodies. It was perhaps in anticipation of this (and doubtless also in response to the national political debate surrounding the passage of the ERA in 1988) that the autumn 1988 parent governor elections were contested in about half of primary schools and three-quarters of secondary schools, with energetic contests and substantial polls in a significant minority of schools.[11]

Governing bodies are still at the beginning of acquiring their new powers and learning how to exercise them. It remains to be seen, for example, how widely they develop executive organs of their own, or delegate matters to heads and other staff. It is clearly part of the ERA strategy that parental influence within schools should focus on and through the governing bodies. Yet the formal machinery for making governing bodies responsive to parents as a whole is slender: 4-yearly election of a minority of the membership, plus an annual formal report.

The other facet is the informal processes by which parents influence governors, and the school more generally: the instruments, orchestration and 'tone' of voice. In almost all schools, it is only a minority of parents who are active; on the other hand, where there is an active minority of parents, their number will often be many times more than the number of elected parent governors. These may seek other fora from which to bring influence to bear; it may be, for example, that one indirect effect of the ERA will be to invigorate PTAs and make them seek a part in substantial decisions.

It is important to remember that parents differ greatly in their attitude to expressing voice and wielding political influence. Some, perhaps most, recoil from it, or experience it as a cost. For others, the element of public service involved, and the opportunities it offers for ethical or ideological pronouncement, make it an enjoyable benefit (see Hirschman, 1981b). This taste for certain types of voice underpins most systems of unpaid representative local government; as a factor in school governance it is likely to be amplified both by the ERA's enlargement of schools' autonomy, and its accompanying rhetoric of parent power and choice.

However, even the majority of parents who are not active (i.e. who experience sustained voice as a cost exceeding its probable benefits) have views, at least on major issues – as the very high polls in early ballots on opting out demonstrated. One further possibility this raises is that of a systematic divergence of preferences between an activist (and perhaps ideologized) minority, and an inactive majority. The main corrective mechanism for this in the ERA is exit, i.e. switching to another school. However, for the individual family this is also very costly. In such a situation it is possible that parent governor elections might come to serve as a secondary channel for a 'silent majority'.

More generally, the tones of voice employed may be expected to shift. The rhetoric of choice, for example, may lead to more acrimonious complaints from parents, and may counteract parental fears that their child will suffer if they complain too vigorously. Conversely, staff may respond differently to criticisms if they fear vociferous exits or falling rolls. These shifts in tone of voice, however, along with the other changes in the micro-politics of school organizations, will be various and often subtle. It may be that the researchers best able to study them are those who already had long-term qualitative studies of individual schools in place before the ERA came into force.

Conclusion

The ERA strategy for the state-funded school system aims to meet parental wishes better through both improvement of schools and greater diversity between them. As far as diversification is concerned, many of the ERA's critics agree with its supporters that more open enrolment and opting out will produce greater heterogeneity between schools, though they regret this rather than welcome it (compare, for example, the comments of the Centre for Policy Studies and the National Union of Teachers on religious or cultural differentiation between schools, in Haviland, 1988, pp. 105–7, 131). Against this, however, is some empirical evidence that there may also be homogenizing effects. For example, a study of the long-term results of open enrolment in primary schools in suburban Massachusetts (Galluccio-Steele, 1986) found that it decreased educational diversity, and that one reason for this was that competition produced more innovation-copying.

As far as the ERA strategy for improving the generality of schools is concerned, this *requires* that schools that are relatively unpopular should, in general, be able to change so as to gain popularity. The strategy also *implies* that an important component in schools' improvement will be parents' involvement in their activity and governance. This need not be so. Many heavily over-subscribed fee-paying schools restrict parents to fund-raising and ceremonial occasions, and their example may explain the small representation of parents on the governing bodies of the government's proposed City Technology Colleges. However, the traditions and cultures of modestly performing LEA schools with low parental involvement, now being jolted into financial and administrative autonomy, are very different from those of successful fee-paying schools; the crucial questions for the ERA strategy are whether their heads and staffs (and governing bodies) will seek ways to reinvigorate them, and if so how. If they fail to do so, this raises the prospect of a vicious hierarchy of schools, from those patronized only by parents who care little about schooling and opt merely for geographical convenience, up to popular schools which are permanently over-subscribed (and perhaps practise significant selection).

The possibility of such a hierarchy of schools is one of the dangers pointed to by those who have criticized the ERA as socially and educationally divisive. Another is the danger that competition for pupils and revenue will disintegrate valuable traditions of co-operation between schools. However, there is one important feature of the ERA that will tend, in the long term, to bring schools together. Hitherto most schools have had to negotiate on an individual basis with their LEA for extra resources, usually above some minimum set by pupil–staff formulae. But, from 1990, when LEAs have settled their formulae for sharing their 'aggregated schools budget' among their schools, they cannot make large short-run changes to them. However, what will change – every year, and as an explicit political decision of the local authority – is the size of the overall schools budget. All schools, and their staff and parents, will have an interest in the largest possible increase in the budget. The very fixity of the formula-funding which central government has imposed on LEAs may create the conditions for powerful LEA-wide co-alitions, uniting schools, staff and their unions with many parents and their organizations, and supported by LEA officers, which are aimed at pressuring local authorities to increase their schools budgets. Thus this particular national strategy for increasing consumer sovereignty may – unlike, for example, council house sales, the deregulation of professions or privatiz-ations of nationalized industries – have the paradoxical effect of bringing consumers and suppliers together to make greater claims on public spending.

Notes

1 For a useful outline of the ERA and its political background, see Maclure (1988). A lawyer's helpful precis of the Act can be found in Liell (1988, pp. 1–58). Further details of the ERA's application to schools were laid down in DES circulars. The ERA's provisions for schools apply only to England and Wales; Scotland and Northern Ireland are subject to separate legislation.
2 There are some secondary differences in the application of the ERA to LEAs' own schools and the voluntary (mainly church) schools financed by LEAs. These do not affect the central arguments.
3 The Conservative Family Association (Haviland, 1988, p. 132) welcomed the proposals in the Bill, but only as an approximation to a system of vouchers.
4 *The Independent*, 2 February 1989, p. 19.
5 On patterns and motives of parental choice, see also: Stillman and Maychell (1986) for England; Petch (1986), Raab and Adler (1987) and Adler and Raab (1988) for Scotland. The recent literature on school choice in the US is considerable; it grows out of earlier discussions of voucher programmes. See e.g. Galluccio-Steele (1986), Oakley (1985), Schwartz (1986), Scott (1983) and Stoothoff (1985). For

surveys, see Raywid (1985) and Zerchykov (1987). Murnane (1986a) discusses problems of enlarging choice in American public school systems.

6 Jowett and Baginsky (1988), a National Foundation for Educational Research report based on a questionnaire survey of LEAs during 1986–7, gives an indication of the extent and variety of parental involvement in schools.   ·

7 Strictly speaking, these considerations (or most of them) apply to the individual's decision whether to exit or stay. But staying is a condition of voice.

8 *The Times Educational Supplement*, 2 December 1988, p. 4, and 12 January 1989, p. 12.

9 Monitoring one Open University course assignment ('Write a 2000 word account of your career in teaching') has yielded a wealth of anecdotal, but I think candid, examples where 'turning round' an indifferent school (or department) is seen as an important accomplishment in a teacher's career.

10 For a discussion of parents as 'citizen-consumers' in education, from the standpoint of the British consumer movement, see Woods (1988).

11 *The Times Educational Supplement*, 21 October 1988, p. 14.

References

Adler, M. E. and Raab, G. M. (1988). 'Exit, choice and loyalty: The impact of parental choice on admissions to secondary schools in Edinburgh and Dundee'. *Journal of Education Policy*, **3**(2), 155–79.

Arnott, R. and Rowse, J. (1987). 'Peer group effects and educational attainment'. *Journal of Public Economics*, **32**(3), 287–305.

Ashworth, J., Papps, I. and Thomas, B. (1988). *Increased Parental Choice: An Economical Analysis of some Alternative Methods of Management and Finance of Education*. London, Institute of Economic Affairs.

Ballion, R. (1986). 'Le choix du college: Le comportement "eclaire" des familes'. *Revue Française de Sociologie*, **27**(4), 719–34.

Brown, M. *et al.* (1985). *No Turning Back: A New Agenda from a Group of Conservative MPs*. London, Conservative Political Centre.

Cohen, M. D., March, J. G. and Olsen, J. P. (1972). 'A garbage-can model of organizational choice'. *Administrative Science Quarterly*, **17**(1), 1–25.

Galluccio-Steele, F. M. (1986). 'Choice and consequences: A case study of open enrolment in the Acton, Massachusetts public schools'. Ed.D. dissertation, Harvard University.

Haviland, J. (1988). *Take Care, Mr Baker*. London, Fourth Estate.

Hirschman, A. O. (1970). *Exit, Voice and Loyalty: Responses to Decline in Firms, Organizations and States*. Cambridge, Mass., Harvard University Press.

Hirschman, A. O. (1981a). 'Exit, voice and loyalty: Further reflections and a survey of recent contributions'. *In* A. O. Hirschman, *Essays in Trespassing*. Cambridge, Cambridge University Press, pp. 213–35.

Hirschman, A. O. (1981b). 'Exit and voice: Some further distinctions'. *In* A. O Hirschman, *Essays in Trespassing*. Cambridge, Cambridge University Press, pp. 236–45.

Jarvis, M. G. (1986). 'Parent choice behaviour in a voluntary school desegregation plan'. Ed.D. dissertation, Southern Illinois University.

Jowett, S. and Baginsky, M. (1988). 'Parents and education: A survey of their involvement and a discussion of some issues'. *Educational Research*, **30**(1).

Liell, P. (ed.) (1988). *Education Reform Act 1988*. Special Bulletin of The Law of Education, 9th edn. London, Butterworth.

Maclure, S. (1988). *Education Re-formed: A Guide to the Education Reform Act 1988*. London, Hodder and Stoughton.

Murnane, R. J. (1986a). 'Family choice in public education: The roles of students, teachers and system designers'. *Teachers College Record*, **88**(2), 169–90.

Murnane, R. J. (1986b). 'Comparisons of public and private schools: The critical role of regulations'. *In* D. C. Levy (ed.), *Private Education: Studies in Choice and Public Policy*. Oxford, Oxford University Press, pp. 138–52.

Oakley, H. T. (1985). 'Parental choice of elementary schooling alternatives in an affluent suburban community'. Ph.D. dissertation, Ohio State University.

Orbell, M. and Uno, T. (1972). 'A theory of neighbourhood problem solving: Political action versus residential mobility'. *American Political Science Review*, **66**.

Petch, A. J. (1986). 'Parental choice at entry to primary school'. *Research Papers in Education*, **1**(1), 26–47.

Raab, G. M. and Adler, M. E. (1987). 'A tale of two cities: The impact of parental choice on admissions to primary schools in Edinburgh and Dundee'. *Research Papers in Education*, **2**(3), 157–76.

Raywid, M. A. (1985). 'Family choice arrangements in public schools: A review of the literature'. *Review of Educational Research*, **55**(4), 435–67.

Rusbult, C. E., Johnson, D. J. and Morrow, G. D. (1986). 'Determinants and consequences of exit, voice, loyalty and neglect: Responses to dissatisfaction in adult romantic involvements'. *Human Relations*, **39**(1), 45–63.

Schwartz, P. B. (1986). 'Expressed reasons for parental choice of private schooling'. Ed. D. dissertation, Columbia University Teachers College.

Scott, C. P. (1983). 'Parental choice behaviour in school selection'. Ed. D. dissertation, Columbia University Teachers College.

Sharp, E. B. (1984). '"Exit, voice, and loyalty" in the context of local government problems'. *Western Political Quarterly*, **37**(1), 67–83.

Stillman, A. and Maychell, K. (1986). *Choosing Schools: Parents, LEAs and the 1980 Education Act*. Windsor, NFER-Nelson.

Stoothoff, J. L. (1985). 'A study of high school selection by parents in the South Colonie central school district of Albany, New York'. Ed. D. dissertation, State University of New York at Albany.

Thomas, H. (1988). 'Pupils as vouchers'. *Times Educational Supplement*, 2 December, 23.

University of Glasgow (1986). 'Summary of "Parental Choice of School in Scotland"', the public report of the Parental Choice Project'. Glasgow, Department of Education, University of Glasgow.

Weick, K. E. (1976). 'Educational organizations as loosely coupled systems'. *Administrative Science Quarterly*, **21**, 1–19.

Woods, P. (1988). 'A strategic view of parent participation'. *Journal of Education Policy*, **3**(4), 323–34.

Young, D. R. (1976). 'Consolidation or diversity: Choices in the structure of urban governance'. *American Economic Review*, **66**, 378–85.

Zerchykov, R. (1987). *Parent Choice: A Digest of the Research. Parent Choice and the Public Schools: Volume 1*. Boston, Mass., Institute for Responsive Education.

6

Democratized primary school government: Conflicts and dichotomies

Christine Pascal

Over the last two decades in many modern industrial countries, large amounts of money, time, energy and human capital have been invested in setting up various kinds of school council, aimed at promoting greater public, parent and teacher involvement in the government of schools. In Britain, in particular, the wider changes in society have led to a reassessment of the structure of the system of school government and a widespread demand that educational institutions are made more accountable and organized in a democratic manner. [. . .]

Throughout this period, research into school governing bodies has been developing steadily, but there is still a scarcity of empirically grounded studies which show how the reforms have worked out in practice. As a contribution to knowledge in this area, a research project (Pascal, 1986) which investigated how a system of democratized primary school governing bodies was operating after 3 years' experience was conducted from 1981–5 in Birmingham. Data was gathered, mainly by questionnaire, interview and observation, from educationalists, administrators, politicians and the public with an interest or involvement in the system. The results of this study were generally optimistic, showing that primary school governing bodies in Birmingham, in which parents were prominent, were making a valuable contribution to the functioning of the system as a whole by acting as a link with the local community and local education authority (LEA), as an advocate of the school and as a first stage in the accountability process. However, a number of structural and administrative constraints were found to be inhibiting their effectiveness and influence, e.g. poor communication, lack of information, insufficient resources and inadequate facilities.

An important feature of the Birmingham study was the observation that school governing bodies were operating within a system where there were many conflicting pressures and demands. An analysis of these revealed a number of underlying dichotomies which school governors were having to cope with in order to play a meaningful part in the system. These dichotomies and the strategies employed by school governors to deal with them, have wider implications for those concerned with developing and improving the policy and practice of school government.

Four central dichotomies were identified and these are discussed in more detail below:

1 Élitism versus pluralism
2 Centralization versus devolution
3 Professionals versus laity
4 Support versus accountability

Élitism versus pluralism

It has never been clear whether society becomes more democratic out of conviction or expediency. The education system operates within long-established centres of power and the driving force behind moves to dissipate these have been subject to much debate. In practice, institutions holding power are likely to wait until they can no longer ignore demands for devolving it. The distribution of power within systems of school government has been explained in a number of ways. At one end of the spectrum élitist models have been put forward, and at the other pluralist models.

Élite models of the distribution of power present public institutions as largely dominated by ruling groups. They argue that moves towards democratization in education are due to political necessity rather than egalitarian sentiments. This model sees educational establishments in modern industrial societies with liberal democratic tendencies facing a number of administrative problems, such as training its labour force, maintaining labour discipline, developing quality control procedures and reviewing and updating its policies. The educational establishment attempts to solve these problems by centralized planning and the creation of large public organizations with specific objectives. However, these large organizations suffer from an inherent paradox, on the one hand existing to serve the interests of the population, but at the same time their personnel are forced to make moral judgements about personal areas of people's lives. This leads to feelings of 'powerlessness' and 'estrangement' by the bulk of the population and gives those in control of the organization further problems. In order to operate, the educational establishment must find ways to maintain their executive control over an organization which is large and costly and remote from the public, and also face the problem of gaining sufficient public support for often contentious new policies. Thus, the democratization of school government is seen in these models as the result of the educational establishment acting in the face of a changing social and political climate in order to maintain their authority and control. Potentially challenging interests are incorporated into the system in ways which ensure they do not offer any challenge to the existing structure of power.

This élite model was put forward by Bacon (1978, p. 191) in his account of the democratization of Sheffield school boards. He concluded his study by arguing:

> It is extremely naive to assume that the pressure for greater parent, worker or community involvement in the management or government of schools presents a genuine, spontaneous 'grassroots' activity. . . . Rather, it seems to be apparent . . . that most of the momentum has been generated by a diffuse but, nonetheless, in part, recognisable, metropolitan intelligensia, either employed directly or indirectly, in elite roles within the nation's public education industry.

Also, Beattie (1978, p. 41) in his comparative study of formalized parental participation in Western European countries following the Second World War argued that the move was due to:

> political necessity and in particular the need experienced in different ways by western democracies to legitimise the status quo by defining certain areas within which democratic participation can occur. In my view, the adoption by liberal democracies of formal machinery for consulting and involving parents in education has little to do with the rightness or persuasiveness of the arguments in favour of such innovations; it has a great deal to do with an underlying crisis of confidence in democratic institutions.

Thus, in this model the democratization of school government is seen as a false front behind which the old hierarchy could continue to operate within the same power structure. Élite theory sees reforms in school government to have had little effect on the existing balance of power in the system.

Pluralist models of the distribution of power emphasize the interplay of organizational interests. Here, power is distributed throughout the system between interests which are institutionalized, and the educational establishment acts as final arbiter in decisions. This model allows for an unequal distribution of power with some groups having greater access to the decision-making arena than others, but power is not concentrated in certain unchangeable centres. The issue often determines which groups exert power, and there may be coalitions of groups over certain issues, which may be fleeting or permanent, but act together as a powerful force for that time. Therefore, in this model power is fragmented between multiple groups or interests which may vary over time and according to the issue. Thus, power is seen as being distributed throughout the system and various groups and institutions are able to exert real influence on the educational leaders. This model has been preferred by more recent writers on school government (Kogan, 1984; Howell, 1981).

It is not easy to see where the present system of school government fits with these two ideal type models, but two constructs seem possible. First, that governing bodies are allowed real authority within a system which is essentially élite but is prepared to devolve some of its power in order to maintain élite dominance. Secondly, that governing bodies are part of a pluralist model, to the extent that power is diffused through the system to them and other groups and they are able to contest the decisions of authorities.

The evidence from Birmingham seems to exhibit some elements of both models. Élitists argue that the incorporation of formerly disenfranchised groups into subordinate positions in the formal structure means they are unable to exercise their representative and policy-making functions and are deterred from expressing their dissatisfaction or opposition to those in control. The absence of conflict is seen to confirm this élitist view. However, although governing bodies are in a clearly subordinate position *vis-à-vis* the school and the LEA, a number of features question the adequacy of this position. First, how far the educational establishment can be identified as a unified interest is debatable. Politicians, headteachers, LEA officers in the study frequently expressed differing views and objectives. Secondly, there were examples of governors challenging the decisions and authority of the educational establishment and, in some cases, succeeding, e.g. over the closure of school or the loss of staff. Thirdly, and perhaps most importantly, there was wide acknowledgement on the part of those in control at LEA and school level, of the potential power of governing bodies. Although these powers were largely not employed, they clearly acted as a check on the exploitation of power by the educational establishment whose authority was dependent on the sanction of these representative bodies.

These factors point to a view of school government which acknowledges the dominance of certain interests but within a system which allows for mediation between, and accommodation of, a wide range of legitimate interests. In this way neither a purely élitist or purely pluralistic model is satisfactory. Professional administrators and educationalists represent one, often fragmented, but dominant interest group, but at any one time they will be under challenge from other interests, to which they must respond. The evidence therefore seems to lean towards a neo-pluralist view (Newton, 1976) in which the educational élite retain the balance of power in their favour but are compelled to devolve a significant degree of power to other participants in the system. Those in control have to adjust their actions to a variety of interests and pressures. Decisions are the outcome of the interplay of various organizational interests on the views of the dominant authority.

Which view is adopted as an explanation of the distribution of power in the system of school government has important implications for future policy. Those who see the reforms in élitist terms as a response to a changing social and political climate which threatens the authority of those in control, argue that governing bodies are unlikely to constitute any fundamental threat to the existing balance of power. Or if they do, they will be abandoned in favour of more centralist and overt forms of control. Those who see the reforms as a response to a genuine wish for involvement by a pluralism of interests are more optimistic for the future. They believe the social conditions which brought these reforms will continue and with time will stimulate more effective participatory development and a more equitable distribution of power. A neo-pluralist view has other implications. Here, the interaction between various groups and institutions provides a forum for the expression of alternative demands and perspectives. All formally represented interests are regarded as legitimate and, where the issue requires, have the potential power to influence those in control to respond to them. However, the numbers, commitment and experience of an interest group determines the power it is able to wield. Implicit in this is the belief that by increasing the investment of participants in these determinants of power, it is possible for groups to increase their influence and authority within the system.

In short, the evidence seems to indicate that the developing power structure in school government is not adequately explained in 'élitist' terms. There is a significant amount of authority and power vested outside the dominant, controlling interests. A purely 'pluralistic' explanation is not adequate either, as power is not diffused between the various interests in the local system. A 'neo-pluralist' perspective which allows for the domination of one interest but where significant power is distributed between a pluralism of other interests seems a more satisfactory description of how many of the participants in the Birmingham system viewed their role and effectiveness.

Centralization versus devolution

There are currently two opposing forces at work in the education system; the move devolving a number of areas of decision making to as local a level as possible and the tendency to develop more centralized planning and management procedures to cope with the situation of economic recession and privation.

Devolution of decision making and control offers a number of benefits. It answers the demands for more participation and involvement, it allows policy to become more responsible to local needs, it opens up a greater range of talents and resources, it reduces feelings of alienation and it allows a greater diversity of services to be made available. The advantages at local and national level have clearly been factors in the devolution that has taken place.

However, there are a number of problems with devolution which together with the tighter economic situation are working to limit further movement away from the centre. Devolution brings with it a conflict of loyalties for those bridging the gaps, problems of definition and jurisdiction between central and local bodies, the need for open channels of communication and an increase in administrative costs.

Viewed in these terms, the current trend towards centralization and the consolidation of control by government is significant. The 'power-sharing' partnership of local and central government, set up in 1944, is being increasingly eroded at the expense of local bodies and in favour of central authorities. It has been strongly argued that the amount of discretion left at local level is now so small, and the weakening of local democracy has gone so far, that education could now be termed 'nationalized' (Alexander, 1982). Moreover, the present social and economic climate (i.e. falling school rolls, increasing curriculum control, the economic recession, etc.) make it unlikely that a reversal of this process of centralization will take place in the foreseeable future. These developments are interesting when weighed against Bacon's (1978) prediction that if the democratization of school government became problematic, the government would revert back to a tighter, more centralized system of control. Is this indeed what is happening?

Recent events reveal a number of contradictions. On the one hand, the multiplicity of governing bodies and the official movement towards giving them greater powers seem to imply a considerable measure of local initiative and control. On the other hand, increasing central control of finance and curriculum seems to imply a large measure of supervision from the centre. These contradictory trends have not gone unnoticed and have caused current government proposals to strengthen and enlarge the powers of governing bodies to be viewed with suspicion. It may be argued that they are a further attempt by those at the centre to undermine the local centres of power, i.e. LEAs and schools, and by doing so reinforce their own position. By failing to address the real obstacles to governing bodies acquiring a firm power base while at the same time attacking the authority of schools and LEAs, power becomes diffused at a local level, and the chance of any challenge to a centralized power structure is diminished. A limited amount of devolution at local level can therefore be seen as a method of bolstering up an overall movement towards greater centralization in the system.

The place of governing bodies in the struggle for power at national and local level, and between the two opposing trends of centralization and devolution, remains ambivalent. It is doubtful whether central government or LEAs will be prepared to yield much more in terms of control of planning, budgeting or curriculum to local representative bodies like governing bodies. Yet the demand for more involvement, a greater say in decision making and more local control will obviously continue. The reconciling of these two contradictory forces will have important implications for the future position of governing bodies in the education system.

Professionals versus laity

Professionalism is increasing absolutely and qualitatively in modern industrial societies, but there is growing evidence of challenges to the autonomy of professionals in all fields by those who use their services, e.g. physicians, lawyers and teachers. This has placed pressure on professionals from both within and outside their ranks. Conflict between professionals and non-professionals (laity) is not a new phenomenon, yet the more recent growth in consumerism has been felt acutely in education. The reform and democratization of school governing bodies which has occurred in the last two decades was a direct outcome of the growing pressure on educational professionals from their clients. However, the evidence from Birmingham and elsewhere illustrates that the reforms in school government to date have not resolved the conflict between professionals and laity in education.

Governing bodies are therefore faced with reconciling the demands of professional and lay interests at two levels: first, within the governing body itself, which is a mixture of professional and lay members; and, secondly, between the governing body as a whole and the school it governs. There is a potential for conflict at both levels, as these two interests have different, and sometimes opposing, aims, purposes and approaches to the issues they jointly face.

Within the governing body we may broadly see LEA governors, teacher governors and the headteacher as 'professionals'. Parent governors and co-opted governors may be viewed as 'laity'. The Birmingham research evidence (Pascal, 1986) showed that each see their role differently. Lay governors tended to see their purpose in a number of ways including monitoring the school, providing an alternative opinion, linking the school and community and providing support – their focus was essentially school-based. Professional governors had varying interests but generally shared common views about the specialist nature of educational work and tended to have a much broader view of their role as part of a wider system of education. At present, the work of governing bodies reveals a resistance to governors becoming more involved in the specialized 'educational' concerns. This reflects the dependence of lay governors on 'professional' members for information, advice and access which allows the professionals to control what issues the governing body is able to tackle. However, it was also evident that 'lay members' were able to influence the 'professionals' to a certain extent by making them account for what is being done in the school system and ensuring that their reactions were noted. Despite this, within the governing body, the 'professionals' generally continue to be the dominant interest.

The relationship between professionals and laity at the second level (between the school and the governing body) generates further problems. It is difficult for part-time amateurs to govern full-time professionals in a meaningful way. Education is an increasingly specialist domain in which developments and innovations constantly appear. However, the evidence reveals that the importance of the parent and community contribution is widely acknowledged and changing circumstances mean professionals now have to 'sell' their services to the population and tailor provision to some extent to the views of their clients. The case for lay involvement at institutional level is a strong one. It reflects the belief that the public should have a voice in the way educational institutions are conducted in order to protect them from domination by professional interests. Although in the past century lay interests have failed to have much influence at this level, recent local and national initiatives have strengthened their role and increased their representation. At school level there is evidence that the balance of power is beginning to alter in favour of lay interests.

Thus, at present, the relationship between professionals and laity in education appears to be in a state of flux, and the potential for conflict between these two interests is clearly evident. Wirt (1981) has produced a development model of conflict between professionals and laity which may be usefully applied to school government as an aid to understanding and description. Wirt describes five stages in the developing conflict:

1 *Quiescence* – a stage where the professionals dominate and the laity are supportive of their dominance.
2 *Issue emergence* – during which complaints emerge on an individual basis as a result of professional definitions of service.
3 *Turbulence* – in which the disaggregated complaints escalate to become an unstructured set of conflict interactions between the professionals and laity over the professionals' definition and execution of the quality of service.
4 *Resolution* – during which issues are removed from the societal agenda to the formal agenda for resolution.
5 *Closure* – the final stage in which resolution results in changes which redefine the professionals' service in accordance with the demands of the laity.

Elements of this model can be clearly identified in the developing relationship between professionals and laity in school government. Although it is difficult to define exactly which stage in the model we are presently at, it is clear that the conflict between professionals and laity in education has not yet been resolved. The indications are that Wirt's description of 'turbulence' will continue to characterize the relationship until the professional interests recognize and respond more fully to the challenges to their autonomy being voiced by the lay interests in school government. There is some evidence that this response is now underway.

Support versus accountability

Governing bodies are expected to pursue a number of purposes, each of which demand different approaches and relationships for them to succeed. School governors are therefore faced with the problem of meeting and reconciling the diverse and possibly conflicting demands being put on them. They are clearly more successful in doing this in some areas than others. There is much potential for conflict in the demands put on governing bodies to be both supportive of the school and also to hold the school to account. This poses important conceptual problems for governing bodies as to whether they should be part of the school – necessary to perform the supportive function; or whether they should be external to it – necessary to perform the accountability function. There is evidence that governors are reluctant to take on any role which might engender suspicion or hostility at school level and are working hard to be seen as part of the school. Also, governors have widely indicated that they prefer a supportive, mediating role above any other (Elliott *et al.*, 1981). Yet governors are increasingly being called upon to perform a role in school accountability and have been given little guidance as to how they should pursue this role without engendering suspicion and threatening the relationships they have carefully built up.

It appears that little thought has been given to the underlying requirements of the various tasks expected of governing bodies. Expecting one body to act as supporters and evaluators at one and the same time, with little guidance as to how to resolve the conflicts inherent in pursuing these functions, is rather a lot to demand. Yet pressure is being put on governors to do just that. The evidence from Birmingham indicates that governors are managing to resolve this dilemma by acknowledging that they have a role to play in monitoring the school but only at a very broad level and equally emphasizing the supportive role. However, if governing bodies are pushed by recently proposed central and local government policy into adopting a more prominent role in the processes of evaluation and accountability, it is likely that the problems in reconciling these two functions will become more evident and acute. It can also only add to the present uncertainty over the position of governing bodies in the local system.

Conclusion

The usefulness of these dichotomies in enhancing understanding of how systems of school government are currently operating is illustrated in the following analysis of the balance of power in the Birmingham system.

It was clear from the Birmingham study that even in a quite radically democratized system of school government, power may continue to be distributed unevenly between the various elements, with governing bodies and particularly their lay members, subordinate to professional full-time bodies and individuals. However, it was also evident that the lay interests embodied in governing bodies are able to exert a subtle but strong influence within the system because of the latent power they possess. Their authority in this respect was widely acknowledged and those in control were clearly accommodating for this in their actions and decision making. Thus, although not radical, a shift had occurred in the distribution of power within the system and this seems to support a neo-pluralist view of the situation, i.e. that there is a dominant interest, but this has to adapt to the pressures of a plurality of legitimate interests and devolve a certain degree of power to them. This perspective explains the current conflict between centralist and devolutionist trends, as in neo-pluralist terms a certain degree of devolution is necessary in order to maintain the control of the dominant interest. The present situation in which governing bodies are apparently being handed more power can therefore be interpreted as a means of diffusing power at a local level. This acts to diminish the chance of any interest challenging the central authority which is at the time increasing its control in key areas of policy and decision making. A further point to be noted here was that although some conflict between the professionals and laity was evident in the Birmingham study, there were indications that governing bodies which embodied an equitable blend of interests engaged in important, appropriate and meaningful tasks could be a vehicle for the resolution of this. Conflict appeared to be generated in situations where one interest was able to dominate an area of mutual concern to the exclusion of the other interest. This especially occurred over 'professionally based' issues such as curriculum development. There was little evidence of conflict between professional and lay interests involved in less 'professionally based' areas, e.g. liaison, where it was possible for them to participate on an equal footing. Thus, the argument that governing bodies are powerless and ineffectual *vis à vis* the professional interest in the system was not borne out in those areas of concern which governing bodies are focusing on in practice.

Bibliography

Alexander, A. (1982). *Local Government in Britain since Reorganisation.* London, Allen and Unwin.

Bacon, W. (1978). *Public Accountability and the Schooling System: A Sociology of School Board Democracy.* London, Harper and Row.

Baron, G. (ed.) (1981). *The Politics of School Government.* London, Pergamon Press.

Baron, G. and Howell, D. A. (1966). *School Management and Government.* London, HMSO.

Baron, G. and Howell, D. A. (1974). *The Government and Management of Schools.* London, Athlone Press.

Beattie, N. (1978). 'Formalized parent participation in education: A comparative perspective'. *Comparative Education*, **14**(1), 41–8.

Becher, T., Eraut, M. and Knight, J. (1981). *Policies for Educational Accountability.* London, Heinemann.

Burgess, T. and Sofer, A. (1978). *The School Governors and Managers Handbook and Training Guide.* London, Kogan Page.

Department of Education and Science (1977). *A New Partnership for our Schools.* Report of the Committee of Inquiry chaired by Mr Tom Taylor. London, HMSO.

Department of Education and Science (1984). *Parental Influence at School: A New Framework for School Government in England and Wales.* Green Paper, Cmnd 9242. London, HMSO.

Department of Education and Science (1985). *Better Schools*. White Paper, Cmnd 9469. London, HMSO.

Elliott, J., Bridges, D., Ebbutt, D., Gibson, R. and Nias, J. (1981). *School Accountability: The SSRC Accountability Project*. London, Grant McIntyre.

Howell, D. (1981). 'Problems of school government'. *In* B. Simon and W. Taylor (eds), *Education in the Eighties*. London, Batsford.

Kogan, M. (ed.) (1984). *School Governing Bodies*. London, Heinemann.

Newton, K. (1976). *The Theory of Pluralistic Democracy*. Oxford, Oxford University Press.

Wirt, F. (1981). 'Professionalism and political conflict: A developmental model'. *Journal of Public Policy*, **1**(1), 61–93.

7

Community education and school:
A commentary

Gordon Mitchell

The notion that the facilities of schools should be more available to all the members of the community in which they are situated is not new. As long ago as the 1920s, Morris, then Chief Education Officer for Cambridgeshire, sought to make schools into community assets in a bid to prevent the depopulation of the rural villages. This initiative to preserve or regenerate community in the face of rapid socioeconomic change has continued. It was a feature of pre- and post-Second World War urban renewal programmes and it has remained so right up to the present, as for example, in the 'planned environment' of Milton Keynes.

Apart from what was seen as a 'general need' to provide community focal points, certain other factors have made it seem 'natural' that schools would be ideal for the purpose.

A large body of research into education in the 1950s and 1960s drew attention to the ways in which the child's educational performance was influenced by factors outside the schools. Especially important was the quality of support for the school by parents. It is now received wisdom that 'improvement' in home–school links has been instrumental in improving the academic attainment of many children in primary and secondary schools.

There have also been changes in the conception of a 'good' (i.e. appropriate) education. Successive national reports in the 1960s emphasized that schools should be as committed to the social, moral and emotional development of their pupils as they are to their academic progress. They also argued that schools should be more keenly aware of the potential afforded by their communities as environmental 'learning laboratories'. Such policies required broad patterns of local partnership between schools and social services and between schools and the world of work. Raising the school leaving age and changes to the school curriculum were reflected in the kind of accommodation provided in new schools. The broadening of the secondary school curriculum, especially in respect of practical skills and the visual and creative subjects, encouraged the growth of purpose-built accommodation: theatres, studios, sports halls.

Certain other facilities such as common-rooms, coffee bars and the like were reckoned more appropriate to the status needs of the many pupils who were virtually adults. The overall effect was to make 'real' adults feel less like intruders in that austere world of desks, blackboards and tables. These altered perceptions of the school's place in the social fabric have tended to develop a more 'active' relationship between school and community.

Further impetus to school–community integration derived from dramatic changes in the demands of the labour market. It has become increasingly clear that the traditional distinction between education and training is inappropriate. The provision of continuing education in some form by way of life skill 'packages' or for 'topping-up' academic attainments, came to be seen as an urgent and indispensable need of young adults.

At the same time, adult education, too, was moving away from the narrowly based programmes of evening institutes. Instead, as Morris had originally envisaged 50 years earlier, it became more widely concerned with at least some of the educational, social and recreational needs of the neighbourhood.

Some local authorities – Coventry, for example, in its policy document *Comprehensive Education for Life* (1984)[1]* – assumed a flexible relationship of schools and colleges of further education to provide a 'seamless web' of educational, vocational and social provision for the neighbourhood.

In summary, then, the coincidence of many economic political and social factors has given impetus to developing uses of schools and colleges in ways other than that for which they were originally created. They have been seen as opportunities growth points – sites for supporting individuals and groups within a given local area. As the Director of Education for Clwyd wrote in 1985:

> . . . the school on its own can never provide the full range of activities and experiences which young people will demand . . . it will be necessary to mobilize the support of the F.E. sector, local employers, trade unionists, leading figures in the community etc. etc. The role of the school will be central to all this but it will no longer be all things to all students, it will assume the function – partly at least – of a control tower/nerve centre/clearing house through which these many-faceted activities will be coordinated.[2]

Economic factors

Educationists tend to concentrate on educational factors in considering change at the expense of political and economic ones. This makes for

*Superscript numerals refer to numbered notes at the end of this chapter.

unbalanced accounting: the influence of economic factors in accidentally bolstering the development of community education must not be under-estimated.

Schools represent considerable public investment: some economists have believed the plant has been under-used for many years. Gradually, schools have become, sometimes grudgingly, sites for adult education classes and youth activities especially in rural areas where the opportunity was taken to build schools incorporating facilities otherwise available only in the large towns. The most common examples have been leisure facilities: often swimming pools provided by merging the capital investment cost of physical education space within the school building with financial support provided by the district council or a grant from the Sports Council. It would be true to say that the driving force in developing co-ordinated facility projects has been the local authorities – there are few examples of cases where they have derived from popular local 'pressures'.

Co-ordinated facilities in primary schools

Some primary schools in rural areas have been built with youth service and/or adult education annexes attached. Commonly, there is no operational relationship between the school and the other services – the additional accommodation makes easier dual (separate) use of the facilities. Local authorities like Leicestershire and Cambridgeshire have developed more comprehensive sets of arrangements. For example, in Leicestershire, Croft C of E Community Primary School provides, on its small campus, a base for a plurality of community needs service: educational, health and welfare and social/leisure. Other authorities, e.g. Oldham, Rochdale and Cheshire, have incorporated community centres into their newest building while some other authorities including those responsible for inner-city schools have focused upon informal programmes of parent education and have either provided purpose-built centres, or adapted existing spare capacity provision for this purpose.

Community schools

A relatively recent educational phenomenon has been the designation by some local authorities of schools as 'community' schools: some schools acquire the designation whether or not they have been officially so labelled. The labels themselves are a source of much confusion. Secondary schools in Coventry, for example, are often described as community schools when their correct designation is 'school and community college' and such a title subsumes a rather different set of practices than that of a community school. More importantly, and deriving from circumstances discussed earlier, community schools are by no means homogeneous in nature. They differ in terms of resource allocation, in management structures and in the extent to which they interact with the local community.

At present, then, 'community school' is a generic term describing institutions which, although primarily designed for the education of children and young adults from 5 to 18, are expected to plan *for* and generate education in its broadest sense for the benefit of the local community.

In an attempt to summarize and simplify the range of practice, it might be useful to offer a modified version of Skrimshire's (1981) typology based on the following three broad categories:

1 The school makes conscious, but limited, attempts to relate to its community, e.g. it seeks to develop home–school links, it encourages community use of school premises when the premises are not required for school purposes.
2 The links between school and community are broadened to include community contribution to school life itself, e.g. parents and other adults taking the role of classroom auxiliaries. School facilities, e.g. library and canteen, are available to the community.
3 The totality of school-based enterprises are planned and co-ordinated so that the school can contribute in whatever ways possible to improve the quality of life in the community.

This categorization of community schools is constrained by the particular organizational methods used to manage them. Particularly important are:

1 *Form of management structure*: there are examples where all the activities on the premises are overseen by a 'school and community association', in effect a school governing body together with members co-opted from 'school-user' groups. Sometimes the head of the school has responsibility for all provision; in other instances the head controls the educational programme, a manager taking responsibility for other community facilities. In other cases, e.g. that formerly employed in the Smallheath Community School in Birmingham, a management team is responsible for separate functions of the site – library, school, adult education, recreation and leisure, etc.
2 *Operational funding*: finance may be via a 'block' grant – the school 'controls' the budget for all activities on the premises. Alternatively, there may be separate estimates and allocations for each type of activity.
3 *Staffing*: school staff may work in different sectors (relatively common). In some instances staff with specialist knowledge, e.g. librarians, may serve as members of school staff. In some schools, e.g. Sutton Centre in Nottinghamshire, teachers recruited to the school staff 'contract' to work one-tenth of their timetable in or with the community. Where schools are combined with other community facilities, problems arise especially in terms of participation and accountability, responsibility and access. There is as yet, no unequivocally satisfactory way of managing co-ordinated facilities: some are administered under informal arrangements which

depend heavily on the ability and willingness of the personnel concerned to work co-operatively.

Future trends

The provision of community education based upon school premises is likely to increase in the future. Some reasons have already been alluded to and it is not intended to repeat them here. One clear problem of a school-based education service is 'How can the needs of a community be identified?' For it is easier to state that the additional uses to which schools are put should contribute to the 'general well-being of the community' than it is to be precise about what the community needs are and, indeed, what the 'well-being of the community' means!

Few schools have the resources to carry out a detailed analysis of its community's needs. Even a sophisticated market research operation might not uncover them and there *are* dangers in the kinds of simplistic surveys that schools can promulgate. For example, people's expectations of what is possible may be governed by their preconceptions about schools and what they believe facilities can offer.

Whatever patterns of service provision becomes commonly accepted, and – as it becomes more general – in order to interrelate educational and other facilities, there will arise a corresponding need to reconsider many questions of controls and regulations. What are the legal liabilities of any school which uses the services, say, of a parent-helper on a school journey and where that parent is seriously injured? Similarly, different forms of public use will bring the buildings into different categories of regulations. Certain activities, for example the production and performance of plays and concerts and the sale and consumption of alcohol, can only be carried out under licence. However, none of these issues is of such intractability as to provide serious hindrance to an evolutionary programme of school–community involvement.

A critical analysis of the school as the site of community education

The school as a facility base for various forms of community education and community use has one obvious advantage: its ubiquity. Even in quite small communities it can function at relatively little cost. Henry Morris endeavoured to convey his aims and ideals of an integrated socio-educational facility through the imagery of building design: especially (and symbolically) significant was his belief that the schools contained within the early Cambridgeshire community colleges were not so obtrusive as to emphasize the domain of the pedagogue and the caretaker! However, the tradition within which most school buildings have evolved puts them squarely in the category including monasteries, mansions and prisons: institutions designed to keep safely separate the dedicated, the privileged or the vicious. Our latter-day primaries and comprehensives – catering for up to 1500–2000 pupils – were apparently designed to cater for all three! One fact is certain, relatively few have been built with broader community use in mind. The examples referred to earlier in the text truly represent a very small minority of schools.

Nor can it be claimed that community schools have as yet demonstrated conspicuous success as multi-purpose educational institutions. The findings of Wallis and Mee[3] are not very encouraging. This is one of the few published empirical investigations into the practice and performance of a small number of community secondary schools. Their work was limited to secondary schools, was restricted by a lack of resources and was specifically limited to an examination of the effectiveness of such institutions as providers of an adult education service. However, many of the comments quoted from their in-depth interviews have the ring of authenticity:

> *Inadequate funding*
> My quarrel with the local authority over community education is that it has been resourced on the old formula of the school plus a little bit more for community education. I believe that you've got to start afresh and devise a new formula when you're using a school over this great length of time . . . it's no good decorating the school once every seven years, it needs to be done much more frequently if you're going to have this multi-purpose use going on from 9 o'clock in the morning until 10 o'clock at night.

> *Shared facilities*
> You can quote the philosophy until you're blue in the face, that equipment is held in common between the school and the community but in the practical situation of very little money available the school quite naturally wants to keep what it's got.

> *Feeling for community education*
> We call ourselves a community school in the hope of pretending we're all one institution – we're not!
>
> Staff haven't got it in their bones that this is one institution.
>
> We have, of course, a responsibility for continuing education but there is not any coherent idea of what it means – we add as we go along.

Wallis and Mee comment that their overall feeling is very strong that school staff have little understanding of the aims of community education and little sympathy for its practice. For example, adults on school premises were sometimes welcomed for such covert advantage the school might take from their presence:

> *Examples of manipulation*
> We have been using adult classes for extra 'O' level groups in language which are not catered for in the school timetable.

A community school is an ideal place for adopting all kinds of ruses because you can bring the children back in an evening, give them a two-hour extra science lesson and call it adult education.

Adults in school classes are a great bonus – you don't get the disciplinary problems and they get their homework in on time.

. . . we had two very difficult girls who caused a lot of trouble. Now the mothers put up with this for one week and then, in the second week they very quietly took those two girls aside, told them a few facts of life, and we didn't have a spark of trouble for the rest of the time.

Encouraging adults as students
It's a rare housewife who can fit in with our timetable.

I reserve the right to ask adults to leave if it doesn't work out.

It's a gesture of goodwill on the part of my staff.'

The authors' conclusions, then, appear to amount to an indictment of community schools as purveyors of adult education and, by extension, of community education. They find that there is little cause for optimism: in terms of life-long learning they say that it seems unlikely that a future generation of independent learners is being developed in community schools. They suggest that community schools will have to overcome 'intractable obstacles' to changes in curricula. They argue that the role needs of head-teachers, community educators and teaching staff in community schools should be researched in order to identify areas of mismatch between needs and previous training and experiences. Finally, they question whether or not community schools are the most effective means of achieving many of the goals that they themselves identify. Can the schools bridge the gaps between:

- School and adult students?
- The organizational and attitudinal differences involved in administering different kinds of service, the one compulsory and full-time, the other voluntary and part-time?
- The tradition of centralized control of schooling and the necessary and flexible variable control required for local community usage?

The picture is probably one with which many community educators, in school or out of it, are familiar – not least by this writer, who concedes the truth of their restrained and cautious criticisms.

However, the fact that community schools have, as yet, only limited success in purveying 'community' education does not mean that they will never be able to do so.

There are a number of considerations which may allow schools to approach 'community' education more convincingly. [. . .] The kind of community education of an all-persuasive kind which was at one time thought capable of developing communities, providing a socially relevant curricula and a base for local radical activists, cannot and will not be delivered through schools. Such goals were always *too* controversial, *too* speculative and simply inadequately thought through.

We need now to consider how and in what ways schools can effectively initiate some *clearly defined* forms of community education. Once such good practices have been identified, then, as Wallis and Mee suggest, they should be carefully monitored and made publicly available. *Community Primary Schools*, edited by John Rennie,[4] is one example of an attempt to make known to a wider audience examples of 'good' practice. Nor should the costs of good practice – financial or otherwise – be glossed over.

Organizational innovation of the kind involved in changing conventional schools to ones which offer close relationships with their communities requires careful planning and preparation. In 1953, Sealy and Wilkinson[5] made a major contribution to the development of community schools by identifying and classifying the difficulties to be encountered. It may be appropriate to recapitulate in abbreviated form, the three sets of issues to be resolved. Specifically, they referred to:

1 *School–community relationships*, e.g. difficulty in determining 'community' and 'community' needs, conflicts of values between school and community, misuse of 'community' surveys, democratic participation of community in school 'life'.
2 *Barriers involving policies and personnel*, e.g. ability of management to introduce policy, nature of experience and training of staff to implement policy, insufficient resources of people and equipment.
3 *Problems involving premises*, e.g. inadequate/inappropriate buildings and sites, recognition that multiple services, even though they use the same site, cannot be administered at the same cost as one of them.

Again, it is easy to provide lists separating out the individual difficulties and problems and even to suggest simple solutions. A major difficulty is that in 'real' situations the problems and difficulties appear simultaneously and impinge on each other. As a consequence, there has to take place a deal of messy compromise and horse-trading that is anathema to a 'natural' instinct for rationality in the conduct of human affairs, a desire for tidiness and clarity. And the whole balancing act is far more complex than is baldly presented. It involves motivation and reward, social psychology and group dynamics, what is euphemistically termed 'creative accounting' and the like. Teacher groups, social service agencies, various 'interested' groups, parent-bodies, all have to be held in some sort of social equipoise. If any ideology of community education is to be effectively expressed from a school base then two factors need to be prominent – a realistic time-scale and a coherent planning process.

A realistic time-scale

It is quite common to hear criticism of community schools or schools with a community 'orientation' because it appears that they have little more to show for their work than 'traditional' schools. The labels are unfortunate and divisive. Is it that one type of school must strive to furnish evidence that it lives up to a predetermined status? Is it that schools which are 'traditional' need to take no account of parents or neighbourhood? Of course not. No school can avoid involvement with its community even if it chooses to do so minimally and reluctantly. Schools have always varied in the collective will and ability of professional and other personnel to develop an education service for the community.

One straightforward way for schools to examine their current position would be to see how and in what ways their network of 'community' education practice matches with the kind of broad schemes produced by Coventry's Community Education Project. It is not suggested that any school – certainly not any primary school with its more limited resources – could and should attempt to establish the range of networks portrayed there. Nor could it be taken for granted that any school scoring highly in terms of the quantity of its links could automatically proclaim its pre-eminence as an 'advanced' base of community education. However, it would enable schools to examine the present extent of their community commitment and identify for the future what was essential, desirable and/or practically possible. Consultative processes need to involve more personnel than school teachers, though it seems sensible that teachers – who, after all, have 'natural' avenues of contact via parents and other official voluntary agencies – should initiate developments.

It needs to be stressed again that many schools do involve themselves in so many ways with their communities. What few of them do is carry out any systematic recording and assessment of community education. One policy to be commended is that of the ex-head of John Gulson Infant School – an inner city, multiracial school in Coventry. Over a period of a decade or more she accounted the activities and dimensions of school–community involvement and analysed them.[6] Some initiatives were failures, some were seen to be effective as short-term projects; others needed modifying by using different personnel; others still were so successful that they became integral to the school's programme.

It would be idle to pretend that the programmes and planning involved in a college of further education bear much resemblance to that of an infant school. But the principles underlying the forms of community education remain markedly similar. Just as communities themselves are richly varied so will be the school or college organizations which provide for and with them. There seems good reason why this accounting of school and college stewardship could be valuable to both school or college and its community.

A coherent planning programme

It might be inferred from the preceding paragraphs that planning for community education is essential. Planning here refers mainly to local planning, but it also has implications at national levels too. If, for example, teachers enter the profession equipped *only* to work with young children, schools can hardly be expected to develop as community education bases. There are other skills essential to teachers as potential support systems for community education – and they involve the development and experience of social skills as well as intellectual ones: a commitment to practice, stamina in the face of difficulties, and an ability to think around contentious issues. Particularly desirable is the ability to relate to adults in a community confidently and sympathetically. In this respect, teaching practice formally, informally or non-assessed ought to have some elements of experience for young teachers in training to work with parents and other adult members of the community.

Planning for school-based community education ought to be an integral part of the school's on-going self-assessment and derive from its present practice(s). The very term 'school-based community education' used here may quite easily give a misleading notion. School-based community education does not automatically and exclusively imply 'on the school premises'.

There is no reason why – as indeed they do now – other locations than schools should not provide 'homes' for certain elements of 'community' education. A school and its personnel should seek to make whatever contribution they can. No school or college can provide a totality of 'community' education for it does not exist.

In summary, the neighbourhood school or college has enormous potential for benefiting its communities quite apart from its physical resources. It has unrivalled access to knowledge of people and places: it has a ready-made network through children's families for informal communication and, through its own position in the establishment, for formal contacts. Within its own precincts, it can – and should – be a frequent meeting place for many purposes by small community groups, and even for really large ones. While it should not attempt manifestly what it cannot achieve, any school, by adopting a 'community education' approach, has a unique opportunity to enhance the social and educational growth of individuals and groups. Schools themselves will benefit quite dramatically from the experience.

Notes

1 Coventry Education Committee (1983). *Comprehensive Education for Life*. Coventry, Coventry Education Committee.
2 *Outlines*, vol. 2. (1985). Coventry, CEDC.
3 Wallis, J. and Mee, G. (1983). *Community Schools: Claims and Performance*. Nottingham University, Dept. of Adult Education.
4 Rennie, J. (ed.) (1985). *Community Primary Schools*. Brighton, Falmer Press.
5 Sealy, M. and Wilkinson, J. A. (1953). 'Overcoming barriers to the development of community schools'. In H. B. Henry (ed.), *The 52nd Year Book of the National Society for the Study of Education, Pt. II, The Community School*. Chicago, University of Chicago Press.
6 *Journal of Community Education*, **4**(3), 1985.

8

Towards the responsive college*†

David Parkes and Craig Thomson

Introduction

This chapter explains outcomes from a major marketing development programme in further education (FE). It concentrates on (a) the creation of systematic marketing management information systems, marketing quality control and market research within college environments, and (b) the management of change and the management of short-term projects to facilitate change. Both of these are relevant to current initiatives concerned with embedding successful marketing structures to relate colleges more closely to their client environment.

Section 1 outlines the objectives of the Responsive College Programme (RCP), its structure, developments so far in the 21 projects, and ways ahead. Section 2 examines specific examples of innovation in quality control, market research and customer communication, but concentrates on a case study of customer communication which has wider significance than its FE context. The creation and refinement of systems and procedures to collect information on present and potential customers and feed this into the decision-making process has been one of the major concerns of the Programme. Section 3 examines the issues involved in successfully launching, implementing and embedding systems derived from 2-year projects.

*Bob Bilbrough, M.E. Adams Chapman and Norman Crowson were involved in the development of the case study reported in Section 2.
† This text is drawn from a range of Responsive College materials held at the Further Education Staff College, Coombe Lodge, Blagdon. A wider range of case studies can be obtained from the RCP bank of information papers held in the college library and from 'Developing the Responsive College', *Coombe Lodge Reports*, **20**(10), 1988.

1. The Responsive College Programme

In the period since early 1986 (the start of the RCP), both the RCP and the further education system as a whole have developed, changed and progressed. *Managing Colleges Efficiently* (DES/LAA, 1987), the Education Reform Act and new conditions of service have dramatically changed the environment.

The RCP was an action programme which has moved in step with the system; the central concern of the Programme, marketing, has become an increasingly important concern of colleges during the life of the Programme. The political and commercial pressures which have pushed colleges in this direction so far are likely to increase. The outcomes from the RCP will hopefully help them to meet the challenge presented by these pressures.

Background

Managed from the Further Education Staff College (FESC) and funded by the Manpower Services Commission (MSC), the RCP has undertaken work in 21 separate local authorities. Ten of these were initially funded for 2 years and have been collaboratively managed by the FESC, the LEA and the colleges concerned. The other 11 (the 'satellites') received funding initially for 1 year and reported directly to the Training Agency (then MSC) with more oblique contact with the FESC. Some projects from both groups have successfully applied for extended funding on the completion of their initial period of work (see Table 8.1).

The 'central' RCP projects were divided into two phases or 'rounds'. The first-round projects (Bedfordshire, Birmingham, Lincolnshire and Sheffield) began work in early to mid-1986 and the second round at the end of 1986/beginning of 1987. Work has been aimed at the development, and the identification and replication of good marketing practice. The model of

Table 8.1   The 'central' projects and satellites

'Central' projects	*Satellites*
Bedfordshire	Buckinghamshire
Birmingham	Calderdale
Lincolnshire	Dudley
Sheffield	Dyfed
	East Sussex
Cleveland	Hereford and Worcester
Doncaster	Kent
Gwynedd	Salford
Lancashire	Somerset
Newham	Suffolk
Strathclyde	West Glamorgan

'responsiveness' adopted by the Programme was a product cycle with four stages:

1. Market research.
2. Product development, selling and promotion.
3. Quality control.
4. After-sales service.

Under the heading of *market research*, both primary and secondary research has been carried out with, in the case of the former, original data being collected and, in the case of the latter, existing sources being drawn on. The aim has been to obtain a better understanding of the characteristics of the marketplace through the identification of general factors likely to influence demand for college courses and services. More specifically, existing client groups and their needs and wants have been researched to gain a clearer perception of the competition which colleges increasingly face.

Work in the areas of *product development, selling and promotion* has centred on the use of the information generated by the information system stages of the product cycle spiral (market research, quality control, after sales). The overall aim is to use this information to ensure that appropriate courses and services are on offer and that potential customers are informed of their existence and persuaded of their merits.

Quality control activity has involved the development of instruments and procedures which allow client-centred monitoring of college courses and services. Central to this has been the canvassing of client (student and employer) satisfaction. It is in this area that there has been most central co-ordination of activity as projects have, for example, adopted and developed instruments used in other areas and have worked together on the development of a central system.

Under *after-sales service* comes the exploration of consequences in terms of progression to employment or further study; determining how useful the college course has turned out to be – how it all worked out in the 'real world'. Least work has been carried out in this section of the cycle with much of what has been done being, logically enough, combined with quality control.

The initial criteria used in the selection of project areas ensured that the work across the four stages of the product cycle, in addition to being carried out in a large number of locations, was carried out in a wide variety of situations. The projects were chosen by the RCP national steering committee to include small and large colleges in rural and urban areas with varying employment levels. Selection further ensured that both metropolitan and shire authorities were involved and that there was diversity in their industrial and commercial bases.

The overall intention of the RCP was to involve clients more fully in the identification and delivery of college courses and services. The key to this is information and a central concern of the Programme has been the development of client-centred performance indicators, consistent with and complementary to those emerging elsewhere, particularly from the work of the Joint Efficiency Study via *Managing Colleges Efficiently* (DES/LAA, 1987).

In addition to the development of performance indicators, it was planned that the outcomes of the RCP should include:

1 Recommendations to national and local bodies and agencies concerning the implications for organizational structures, conditions of service and funding arrangements of the introduction of the product cycle and performance indicators.
2 Useful examples of the implementation of the product cycle and performance indicators at LEA/college level.
3 Training packs with the appropriate material and exercises for use in college, local and regional workshops.
4 A group of experienced and knowledgeable local authority officers, project co-ordinators, college officers and the central team, available to organize and contribute to both national and regional conferences on improving college responsiveness to employer/employee training needs.

General outcomes

The outcomes include tried and tested pro formas for marketing planning and course audits; interview and questionnaire instruments have been designed, tested and developed; computer software for electronic databases and data analysis has been written and developed or adapted from commercially available packages. A further outcome is the development of performance indicators which can be adapted for use across the FE system.

Slightly less tangible are the systems and approaches, based on experience, which the RCP has initiated and identified. Approaches to market research and quality control, for example, and systems within which information collected can be fed into the decision-making process, have been developed, piloted and costed. Also less tangible, but nevertheless capable of being described and illustrated, is the wide range of RCP experience in the 'how to' line: how to produce effective promotional materials; how to assess their impact and appropriateness; how to organize employer meetings, breakfasts, lunches, conferences; how to capitalize on their outcomes.

Perhaps the least tangible RCP outcome of all, however, is its experience in dealing with the central challenges: how to shift the organizational culture, overall approach and atmosphere in a college from a provider-centred, non-marketing stance to a client-centred, marketing one. It is here that organizational structures, conditions of service and funding arrangements come into play as facilitating features or barriers to progress. This issue is taken up in Section 3.

2. Quality control, market research and customer communication

Quality control

Quality control (both in-course and after sales) involves monitoring client-centred outcomes in particular (and to a lesser extent processes). What are the outcomes for students, for example, in terms of qualifications gained, progression to appropriate jobs and courses, etc.? From an employer's point of view, to what extent are employees who are attending courses acquiring appropriate skills, abilities and attitudes? Also, to what extent are vacancies being filled by suitable staff: what has been the college's contribution in this area?

Developments in quality control in the projects have both contributed to, and benefited from, the main quality control work of the Programme which has been co-ordinated from FESC. Centrally co-ordinated RCP quality control activity (including after-sales service) draws information from two main sources: from questionnaires to students and employers and from college records. Information on levels of client satisfaction and on student destinations is provided by way of the questionnaires, whereas completion and qualification rates are drawn from records.

The questionnaires and procedures and the overall system within which they fit are being subjected to continued piloting, review and revision as the Programme progresses. The aim has been the creation of a versatile system capable of providing a wide range of useful information at a variety of levels in the college – principal and management team, course teams/class teachers and marketing personnel.

The system (Thomson, 1988) draws its name from its central concern with the perceptions of students and employers – the Responsive College (SPOC/EPOC) Quality Monitoring System (SPOC/EPOC stands for Student/Employers Perceptions of Colleges).

This development work has been carried out with other quality initiatives in view. For example, close attention has been paid to the information-gathering requirements resulting from the MSC NAFE Student Information Systems project and to the framework of effectiveness indicators established in *Managing Colleges Efficiently* (DES/LAA, 1987). One of the major aims of development has been the creation of a system which is capable of generating performance indicators which are of use both to college management and to teaching staff. The system also aims to provide more detailed information (individual written comments from students and employers, etc.) to teaching staff, an important balance to the 'statistical' output.

The indicators which such a system generates can provide no more than a guide to where there may be cause for satisfaction, congratulation or concern. The logical next step in situations where it appears that more incisive information is required is detailed investigation.

In developing the Responsive College (SPOC/EPOC) Quality Monitoring System, RCP has gone beyond the simple collection of information and looked in detail at how it should be analyzed and reported – the aim being the provision of the right information to the right people in a useful and usable form. The principal and management team, the marketing manager and the course teacher are recognized as all having different requirements in terms of types of information and levels of aggregation. Appropriate analysis procedures and report formats have been developed to cater for the specific requirements at each level.

Market research

Despite there being much useful information and informed opinion, discussion and debate on the development of approaches to market research in further education tend not to be particularly sharply focused. A firmer framework for description and communication is obviously required, if the variety of activities and procedures being developed in market research are to form the basis of an accessible and comprehensible approach.

A step towards this has been achieved by the RCP. Recognizing that market research and quality control are essentially part of the same process of gathering, analyzing and using key marketing information, a framework can be established around the notion of indicators – performance indicators on the one hand, market indicators on the other:

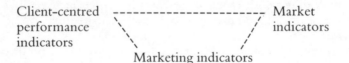

Client-centred
performance
indicators

Market
indicators

Marketing indicators

As in the case of the performance indicators emerging from quality control/after-sales work, market indicators provide broad brush information which can guide management decisions. Detailed further investigation of markets can only be achieved by moving beyond indicators to more incisive investigation, i.e. looking in detail at market segments, client groups, individual clients.

Customer communication

While it may now be a commonplace to state that marketing is not simply selling and promotion, in reality it is aspects of these activities which tend to dominate discussions at conferences, meetings and casual gatherings of college marketing personnel. In rejecting a narrow definition of marketing, the RCP does not suggest that selling and promotion activities are anything other than crucial. However, it is essential for the 'responsive college' to have access to the information necessary to ensure that it is selling and promoting the correct product. Furthermore, successfully carrying out promotion and selling requires sound information to ensure that they can be clearly thought through, thoroughly planned and carefully monitored.

All of the first-round 'projects' work was carried out with the aim of improving the various colleges' capacity to sell and promote themselves. The co-ordinators worked with college staff on promotional materials such as course leaflets, stills photographs, etc.; organized and ran promotional evenings with local employers; analysed current practice and recommended approaches to making contact with employers; looked in detail at enrolment activities and worked on designing and implementing new procedures in this important area of customer contact.

In Sheffield, the RCP carried out research to help it reach a clearer practical understanding of customer care, customer liaison and related areas of activity. This case has wider implications, particularly in the light of the 1988 Education Reform Act, and therefore we have selected it for closer examination.

Lowering the barriers: A case study of customer communication

The development of the customer-focused college was central to the aims of the Responsive College Programme. In Sheffield, the co-ordinators explored a number of customer communication issues. The process of intervention and change in this area which has been taking place (and is continuing) in the Sheffield colleges is described below.

It is not the intention to offer a simple formula for improving the interaction between colleges and their clients. It is recognized that each Authority has its own distinctive operating environment. Sheffield went through a period of considerable change leading to the establishment in September 1988 of six new tertiary colleges.

The Sheffield environment is a turbulent one and this has had a significant impact on the process of change. Nevertheless, the lessons may be generalized and it is hoped that the Sheffield experiences will be useful to those in other Authorities.

Initial research

The Project set out to discover more about customer care, customer liaison and related areas, which are the focus of this case study. Among those whose opinions were sought were employers, the Chamber of Commerce, students, ex-students, potential students, Youth Training Scheme (YTS) managing agents and the MSC. These clients reported a number of barriers to effective communication with further education colleges. The main points raised were:

- low levels of service during the summer when employers and the MSC need information for planning purposes;
- staff unable or unwilling to give information to callers;
- poor customer communication skills;
- inadequate signposting in colleges;
- unfriendly reception areas;
- a shortage of user-friendly course literature;
- lecturers not available for discussion; and
- poor communication procedures – message not getting through.

A telephone survey was carried out by the Project team to try to discover what it was like being on the consumer end of the line. In a random sample responses to calls were logged. Although these were sometimes positive, there were many negative or unhelpful responses with the caller being given no useful information, left to wait for long periods or told to call back later. In the late afternoon or during vacations, responses were particularly unhelpful: 'They've all gone home. There's nobody here!' This pattern is a familiar one, identified by RCP co-ordinators around the country, and Sheffield is far from unusual in this respect.

The issues

The Responsive College Programme team identified four main areas for action aimed at improving the situation:

1 The provision of an information base and user-friendly publicity material.
2 The strengthening of communication channels and the development of roles and responsibilities to support customer care.
3 The development of staff (lecturers, administrative, managerial) attitudes to support the customer-centred organizations.
4 The improvement of staff communication skills.

The Project undertook a number of initiatives to help push these points forward and ensure that the planned action became reality. They set out to:

- promote increased awareness of the importance of these issues;
- work with the colleges to iron out some of the practical problems; and
- persuade college management teams and the LEA to take ownership of some of the more deep-seated problems which had implications for the new tertiary system.

Raising awareness

In pursuit of these ends, the following actions were taken:

1 The Project workers did presentations to college publicity and marketing committees to stimulate an awareness of the difficulties encountered by callers. A YTS managing agent was called in to talk to heads of department

about how and why he had been put off using the colleges. For the most part the heads accepted the criticisms made, although some were quick to point out that a shortage of resources was at the root of the problem.

2 A presentation of the findings of the telephone survey was made to the city's principals and vice-principals. Particular care was taken to identify the colleges' strengths as well as their weaknesses. However, the principals argued that the findings were not relevant because of the sampling techniques used and no apparent progress was made in the matter at senior management level for some time.

3 Lecturers in two colleges agreed to undertake a survey on customer communication in their colleges and present a report to the Project. This fulfilled the dual purpose of stimulating debate among lecturers and providing the Project with a lecturer perspective of the college/customer interface.

4 A video was commissioned showing a client's experiences when contacting an unresponsive college followed by a contrasting response from one with a well-developed customer focus. This was found to be a powerful tool in drawing attention to the importance of:

- tidy, welcoming reception areas;
- systems/procedures for dealing with enquiries;
- a comprehensive course information base;
- positive attitudes by lecturers and administrators;
- training for receptionists; and
- well-developed customer liaison skills.

5 The Project worked with colleges to organize employer events where it was evident that the service was not really 'getting the message through'. Guidelines were therefore drawn up for dissemination in the colleges, to increase awareness of employers' needs and perceptions.

RCP initiatives

A number of initiatives are worth recording:

1 Reception training was carried out. A 2-day course was arranged for administrative personnel of the five colleges acting as the first point of contact, i.e. receptionists and telephonists. It concentrated on demonstrating the needs of callers and improving participants' skills. One of the most useful features was the opportunity it gave staff to discuss some common problems and seek solutions. They displayed a keen desire to improve the service but had strong words to say about the support needed, summarized as follows:

- comprehensive information on courses;
- ability to locate staff;
- improved induction for new front-of-house staff;
- regular updating on new college initiatives;

- better leaflets on courses and college services; and
- more information about other local colleges

It was interesting that the views of this group were reflected in the lecturers' report on communication.

2 Some clients indicated that the traditional prospectus did not give the information they needed. Individual college prospectuses, it was suggested, were not particularly helpful in the city context where travel to each college was possible from all areas. Other clients said that the depth and breadth of information contained did not correspond with their needs.

Three initiatives resulted. The first was the Projects' proposal for the production of one single prospectus for all the colleges, thus releasing resources for specialist publications aimed at particular market segments such as school leavers, employers or women returners.

According to training officers and careers officers it was often necessary to telephone several colleges to obtain course details, which were often incomplete. They suggested that what was needed was a compendium of course information for all the colleges, classified under occupational rather than departmental groupings. The attention of the five colleges' publicity committee was drawn to this and the outcome is the Sheffield Colleges' Directory which is now in use.

Course leaflets were prepared and produced. It was clear that a new approach to course leaflets was required, i.e. that these should be aimed at clearly identified market segments and where necessary give details of city-wide provision. The Project team therefore worked with FE development groups to prepare examples of good practice.

3 Work was carried out on college entrances. The Project team obtained the permission of the principal and worked with the Design Department of one college to improve the reception area. This, it was hoped, would provide a good example for other colleges. The entrance now looks more attractive and is better signposted.

Considerable progress has been made. However, much work has yet to be done in this area to ensure that negative messages are not transmitted to visitors and existing or potential business lost.

The response of policy makers

The RCP team was initially successful in persuading senior managers in all of the colleges that customer care was an area that needed attention. A report on customer communication was prepared but the Authority's senior advisor resigned before dissemination and it was temporarily shelved. The Principals-Designate of the new tertiary colleges have been approached to examine the implications of the key issues with respect to the new institutions.

The senior advisor asked the RCP team to work with college administrators to produce a common application form. There is a proliferation of course application forms across the city, which is confusing for applicants. A draft of the form's content was approved and passed to the Principals-Designate to be transformed into its final 'user-friendly' form.

Attempts were made to persuade colleges of the benefits of improving the service during the long vacation and September enrolment when, it was suggested, opportunities were being lost to communicate positive messages to employers and prospective students alike. The impetus of the post-primary reorganization led to the establishment of an Access and Recruitment Working Party which took over the ownership of these key issues.

Advertising by the Sheffield Colleges has been done on a piecemeal basis and its effectiveness rarely formally evaluated. The Project reported on advertising to the Marketing Panel and suggested that it should take place within a corporate promotional plan, which should itself be rooted within a strategic marketing framework. The view was that until it is known to whom the colleges are communicating, and why, then it is unlikely to be totally effective.

The potential conflict was identified between the colleges' need to promote programmes vigorously and the clients' need for unbiased guidance and counselling. A project paper was prepared on this.

The benefits of a central information point for each college and one for the city was identified as was the post of marketing or information officer to manage customer communication. The heavy resourcing implications appeared to be the main reason for the initial lack of progress in this area.

The nature of these barriers has been communicated to colleges, and decision makers have been made aware of the need to:

- bring front-of-house staff out of their glass cages;
- give greater visibility to black people and mature people at the front of house;
- provide services to attract the general public (area housing office, citizens' advice bureau, college shop);
- locate more customer services at the point of entry (shops, cafeteria, library); and
- meet employers on their terms.

Client groups suggested that enquirers are often inhibited by the hidden messages which confront them at their first point of contact. Women with children, the elderly and black people are particularly vulnerable. The colleges are on campus sites which makes it difficult for people to drop in from the shopping centre. Potential clients who have no interest in education are unlikely to find themselves in a college on any other business. Those who venture in have to make their business known on arrival. At this stage they may be alienated by the bureaucracy or the symbols which confront them at the initial point of contact. It was also felt that employers found the college environment 'unresponsive' to their needs.

Conclusions

Throughout 1986 and 1987 and into 1988, the Sheffield colleges laid the foundation for improving customer communication. Clients are now receiving clearer messages and it is easier for them to get through to the colleges. The changes that have been made are small, compared with those that have yet to take place. However, the lessons learned about the process of implementing such changes will be invaluable in maintaining its momentum.

3. Line management: Making things work

Context and environment

The negotiation of projects' entry into the Programme (1985–6) coincided with the agreement between MSC and the Local Authority Associations that created WRNAFE (Work Related Non-Advanced Further Education) Development Plans. The Programme itself was born out of a perceived need for the FE service to justify its responsiveness to a doubting government. Early in 1989, the impact of the Education Reform Act on colleges of further education is still hazy. For the principals and education officers in RCP, managing is still partially dependent on being able to *grasp the new patterns* in which different sectors of education and training are related to each other. Part of the task of the project co-ordinators was to develop a Management Information System that would help principals and officers *manage the gaps* between colleges and clients, colleges and the Authority, and colleges and competitors, and would assist their understanding of what is actually going on.

The issues of management and ownership are reflected across the 10 projects and the 11 satellites. The relationship between developing a marketing management information system and managing a marketing dimension is crucial to the college and to the authority. The location of the project co-ordinators and their 'clout' was a vital factor.

Their 'credibility' was a necessary factor in managing or influencing the 'embedding' stage. They needed to be in the right place at the right grade with the right backing whether obtaining commitment from staff at course level, influencing WRNAFE planning, or having RCP objectives reflected in college policy.

Organization and structure

What impact has market research and quality control had on internal structures? The answer lies in the development of functional activities: course evaluation, and the establishment of corporate identity together with the acquisition of new types of post-marketing officer, information officer, etc. Specific lateral activities have been developed, modified or improved such as enrolment procedures and employer contacts.

The product cycle as a marketing management information system is likely to shift emphases within colleges and departments rather than offer an exemplary academic structure. The Programme points to the internal reorganization of departments (e.g. catering) rather than major structural reorganization. Most research evidence on structure indicates that it is the *process* of agreeing or understanding that is important and not the *product* of any particular organizational form. There is *no* ideal academic structure.

Management for a Purpose, the report of the Good Management Practice Group (NAB, 1987), suggests that:

> good management practice within efficiency and effectiveness enforces the principles of:
> (a) a conjunction of responsibility and authority;
> (b) the devolution of responsibility to the lowest possible level;
> (c) the location of accountability;
> (d) decision making and accountability to occur within a reasonable time-span.

These were good rules in the location of project co-ordinators as change agents or the college/local authority placing of marketing responsibilities. Because a college is an organizational device for sharing resources among courses which students attend, then, by the criteria above, marketing functions and marketing management information systems require a portfolio distribution of responsibilities with a firm sense of ownership at course level together with a willingness of senior management teams to target problems and to address them.

Role of management

Negotiation with each of the project authorities and colleges has centred on the backing of a line manager. The success of a project package depends largely on its objectives matching the parallel needs from principal or education officer. FESC's focus to monitor, evaluate and support has been important to keep a balance between competing claims on project resources.

In every project college, despite the need to identify 'ownership' and 'what's in it for me?' at every level in the institution, the principal has been the key gateway to managing change. If his or her support is merely lip service, or if there is opposition, then the going is very rough.

Marketing and funding for marketing activities in a market economy are drives affecting education and training sectors worldwide. 'Soft' money funding flourishes. What a successful RCP project offers to the manager is a framework of understanding, a means of implementation and indicators for success.

Administration and procedures

Project co-ordinators believe that durability of change arises from a cumulative series of piecemeal administrative changes that amount to irreversibility. The embedding of systems needs to occur within a college's administration.

College structures split among government (where policy decisions are taken), management (their implementation), and administration (the day-to-day servicing of resourcing decisions). It is the latter that gives the necessary concreteness of routine to otherwise drifting initiatives. 'Freeze, change, refreeze' is a classic shorthand in the management of change and complements the need to bureaucratize. *Procedure provides longevity*.

Conclusion

A number of necessary conditions are required for success. RCP has aims and objectives which have been and are still consistent with local, national and international pressures. Colleges have had to manage mixed-economy institutions: traditional LEA-subsidized education and training for the public good; full cost courses for the private sector; and a third intermediate sector – a category of learning activities subsidized by government agencies somewhere between the public and private sectors.

Success has also been *finance-led*. In Birmingham, Bedfordshire, Lincolnshire and Sheffield, resources have been unearthed from public and private sector sources. Credibility has been earned and developed from specific and concrete achievements consistent with overall aims but taken incrementally.

Changes in attitudes are perhaps the greatest single achievement of the co-ordinators, a factor which uses vast energies and needs to be subsequently sustained in systems. In several projects the operational stage has only been undertaken when the 'attitude changers' have moved on to other posts and left the mopping-up process to their successors whose 'credit' has not been expended.

Consolidation has occurred through the embedding of systems, the development of procedures and the building of continuity via responsibilities in senior management roles. People (principals/project co-ordinators) are important.

References

Department of Education and Science/Local Authority Associations (1987). *Managing Colleges Efficiently*. London, HMSO.

National Advisory Body for Public Sector Higher Education (1987). *Management for a Purpose: The Report of the Good Management Practice Group*. London, NABPSHE. (*Note*: NABPSHE is now the Polytechnic and Colleges Funding Council.)

Thomson, C. (1988). 'Monitoring Quality'. *Coombe Lodge Reports*, **20**(12).

9

Institutions and their local education authority

John Mann

Roll up that map, said Prime Minister Pitt, it will not be wanted these ten years.

Introduction

In its own field, the Education Reform Act is as clear a turning point as Napoleon's triumph at Austerlitz which prompted Pitt's words, the partition of Africa in 1884–5, or the Treaty of Versailles in 1919.

Secretary of State Kenneth Baker has drawn a new map of English education. He has created some new 'states'; the National Curriculum Council, the School Examinations and Assessment Council, and the Curriculum Council for Wales, have sprung from the ashes much as Czechoslovakia and Yugoslavia did in 1919. He has used some familiar terms like 'school', 'college', 'head', 'principal', 'governor', 'local education authority', and 'Department of Education and Science'. But schools, colleges, heads, principals, governors, LEAs and the DES no longer occupy the same positions as they did on earlier maps.

Even more important, the new map shows only some of the boundaries between these new 'states'. Others have still to be drawn. Heads have new duties, governors new powers, and LEAs new functions. In these circumstances boundary management takes on a new significance. This chapter puts up some markers for heads and governors who want to make the most of their new relations with their LEA.

New ways of managing the education service

The Education Reform Act does not stand alone as a one-off piece of legislation. It is the culmination of a decade of change which includes the

Education Acts of 1980 and 1986, and the Education (Grants and Awards) Act of 1984. Together with Training Agency (Manpower Services Commission) grants for the Technical and Vocational Education Initiative and work-related further education, and Department of Employment grants[1]★ for strengthening the Careers Service, these constitute a revolution in how the public education system is managed.

The Education Reform Act embodies even more radical measures which have enormous implications for schools, colleges and LEAs. These measures include the National Curriculum, open enrolment, local management and grant-maintained status.

At first sight the Education Reform Act (ERA) seems to raise doubts about the need for LEAs. They are squeezed between institutional autonomy and central controls like those on general and specific grants, the curriculum and pupil assessment, and teachers' conditions of service. For all that, ERA may come to be seen as a charter for local government. In prescribing the powers and duties of the Secretaries of State, governing bodies and heads, the Act also clarifies the role of LEAs.

When the dust settles they will be seen to have distinct and well-defined responsibilities for managing the education service. Acknowledging and using the LEAs' powers to their own advantage will be one of the hallmarks of successful heads and governors.

Local management of schools and colleges

The Education Reform Act builds on foundations carefully established in earlier measures. Local management is based on the 1986 Education (No. 2) Act which reconstituted school governing bodies and gave them new powers.

Circular 7/88 (Para. 9) on the *Local Management of Schools* highlights the government's aims in introducing this scheme and the parallel scheme for college management. 'Local management of schools' represents a major change in the management of children's education in England and Wales. Needs-based formula funding and the delegation of financial and managerial responsibilities are key components of the government's strategy for raising standards of teaching and learning in schools, and colleges.

Local management means that many powers hitherto exercised at town and county halls will now be exercised at schools and colleges. But no school is an island, and schools will have not one but many different kinds of links with their LEA. Even those which opt for grant-maintained status will have a close interest in their LEA's funding formulae, its support systems for pupils, and other LEA services the school may wish to buy. School governors and heads will need to distinguish clearly between these different kinds of link

★ Superscript numerals refer to numbered notes at the end of this chapter.

in order to provide the best service for their community and derive the greatest possible benefits for their school.

Schools and their environment

Models from the armed forces, engineering and cybernetics throw some light on how to run good schools. But examples from the natural world are even better. Schools have more in common with living organisms than with mechanical or electronic systems. Like plants, they draw energy and sustenance from their environment, and give back fuel and nourishment. Unlike plants, they have the capacity to manage their environment purposefully.

Each school and college determines its own aims, and tries to use its own environment to serve those aims. For most of these institutions the LEA is the largest single feature in their environment, their Ayers Rock. How can they use this monolith to achieve their aims?

The LEA is a potential source of much more energy and sustenance than the funds it must provide. Here is a source of information about local developments, educational developments elsewhere, and new ideas. Here is the most accessible opportunity to engage in local and national development projects, to feel part of an enterprise which transcends the interests of a single school. Here is a source of expert advice on matters ranging from curriculum and assessment to staff and financial management. Here is the agency for staff and governor training. Here is the agency best placed to give discreet, informed assessments of a school's performance. And here, among councillors, officers and inspectors, are potential allies in raising the school's performance and its standing in the community.

It would certainly be worth discussing with councillors, officers and inspectors their various perceptions of their own new functions. The Council's strategic functions, the Chief Officer's statutory right to inform and advise governing bodies, the LEA's duty through its inspectors to monitor and assess – all are now more clearly defined than hitherto. In future, schools and colleges are more likely to look to council officers from the education and other departments for professional expertise rather than authoritative interpretations of council policy or access to resources.

How to influence the LEA

Through their governors and heads, schools have many opportunities to influence their LEA. The first requirement is to know the 'enemy'. Governors and heads should make sure they see the most important Education Committee papers, and attend the key debates. If possible, they should put themselves where the action is. Most LEAs have various working parties, advisory committees and steering groups, on matters ranging from inservice training, to TVEI, work-related further education, special needs, and governor training. Some have a forum for consulting representative governors. Membership of groups like these ensures that a school is well informed, and that its own particular needs and potential contribution are known.

The next requirement is to keep potential allies in the picture, to make sure influential members and leading officers see the school's newsletter, with its constant reminders of what the school is achieving, and what its concerns are.

In some respects a school's relations with its LEA are governed by statute. An LEA must consult every governing body about its proposals for local management. Schools have an opportunity to suggest amending the draft formulae to ensure, for example, that the age weightings are wholly appropriate and fair, and that other factors such as the numbers on roll, social deprivation and the state of the buildings are given enough weight. In many LEAs, governing bodies, heads and other staff will each have opportunities to contribute also to the debate about how their LEA should use the relatively small part of its schools budget which is not distributed to schools. It is for the governing body to put the school's corporate view on these matters to the LEA. This process gives schools one finger on the tiller of LEA policy. It also puts the quality of their contribution on display.

Their response to other LEA initiatives will have the same effect. The governors are required for example to consider the LEA's curriculum policy, and may either adopt it or give their reasons for modifying it. The kind of response they make may depend on what kind of issue the LEA has raised. They might say perhaps that the school would provide double science for all its pupils if it had sufficient laboratory accommodation, that they intend to modify the LEA's homework policy, or that they cannot accept the LEA's suggestions on sex education. They may be able to advise the LEA what measures are needed to implement its policies, or how the policies could be improved.

In certain circumstances, governing bodies may try to influence an LEA by governing body resolutions or public campaigns against the LEA's proposals. Campaigns against proposals to close or merge schools, or proposals to change their character, perhaps by creating a tertiary or sixth-form college, are familiar enough. With local management, governors may feel free to campaign on more general educational issues, such as funding levels and curricular policies, or to launch marketing campaigns for their schools.

It is a matter for fine judgement whether a school's interests are best served by supporting or opposing the LEA. Short-term tactical considerations and long-term strategy may not always point the same way.

The school as LEA agent

The previous section emphasized the school's independence of its LEA. This independence extends even to circumstances where a school or college is acting as the LEA's agent. This is the case whenever a governing body enters into a contract to spend part of its delegated budget. In exercising these powers, governors have much freedom. Under local management, schools and colleges will be able to buy goods and services wherever they see fit, taking into account quality and convenience for the school as well as price. This applies also to services which are subject to competitive tender, such as grounds maintenance, vehicle maintenance, cleaning and catering.

If schools and colleges choose to be covered by an LEA contract, they may specify the standard of service they require and the LEA should include this in its tender documents. If the governors require additional services they may publish their own specification and make their own arrangements.

Some schools may be able to negotiate for certain services better terms than the LEA can secure. What an LEA's schools might consider collectively is whether in the long run their individual interests are most likely to be best served by acting separately or as a group through their LEA. What seems clear is that the potential benefits of collective bargaining might be eroded if some schools were to act unilaterally in what seemed to be their own immediate interests. The best solution may lie in a curious role reversal with the LEA acting as agent for a co-operating group of schools.

The school or college as employer

Establishment and selection

Under the Education Reform Act governing bodies will exercise almost all an employer's functions, with few of the employer's responsibilities (see Circular 7/88, paras 156–72). The governors will decide how many people should work at the school, and the balance between teachers, technicians, welfare assistants, caretakers and other categories of employee. This provision will not include school meals staff unless provision for meals has been delegated to the school. For new non-teaching staff, governors will be able to specify the duties to be performed and the appropriate grade within the range currently applicable to employment with the LEA. They will exercise any discretion, such as the starting point on a scale, which the LEA has over remuneration.

The governors will decide their own selection procedures, subject to a requirement that they must consult the head and the Chief Education Officer, and must consider the Chief Education Officer's advice whether or not they have asked for that advice. In selecting staff, governors are bound by the statutory provisions on race and sex discrimination, but 'they will not be bound by non-statutory LEA policies relating to selection' (Circular 7/88, para. 160), a matter which may cause concern in some LEAs with well-developed selection procedures and policies.

When the governors have made their decision, an LEA must appoint the person selected by the governors unless the person concerned is unable to meet the statutory requirements relating to qualifications, health, physical capacity or conduct.

Industrial relations

One of the most remarkable aspects of the Education Reform Act is how it moves the focus of industrial relations from town and county hall to school and college.

Grievances and discipline

Even more startling is that schools and colleges will determine their own grievance and disciplinary procedures, subject only to a requirement that the Chief Education Officer and the head should be present at all stages when a dismissal is being considered. Either the governors or the head may suspend on full pay anyone who works at the school, but only the governing body may end a suspension. There is, curiously, no provision in the Education Reform Act for an LEA to suspend or dismiss anyone employed at a school or college. The arrangements for dismissal have to include an opportunity for an individual to make representations, and to appeal, prior to a decision to dismiss being transmitted to the LEA. The LEA must implement within 14 days a governing body's decision to dismiss.

A governing body will also have the right to determine the size of any payments in excess of the statutory or contractual obligations. The LEA must meet these and other costs arising from resignations, dismissal or premature retirement. The LEA may not charge these costs against the school's budget share unless the authority has some good reason to deduct some or all of the cost from the school's budget. The Circular suggests (Circular 7/88, para. 167) that excessively high payments or the probability of a dismissal being found unfair by an industrial tribunal might be regarded as good reasons. But an LEA's 'no compulsory redundancy' policy is not a 'good reason'.

Negotiations

Governing bodies will negotiate with trade unions, and though they must recognize unions which their LEA recognizes, they will be free to recognize other unions as well. Some school governors may wish for example to recognize the Professional Association of Teachers, and some tertiary college governors may wish to recognize unions of school teachers.

Both in setting up their disciplinary and grievance procedures and in dealing with specific cases, governors may be asked to negotiate with trade unions. Trade unions may also be concerned with establishment matters, job descriptions, conditions of service, and health and safety. They would probably be concerned if governing bodies were to exercise their power to require the removal from the premises of anyone employed by the authority to work at the school, and to appoint someone else to do the work. This covers people in Council Direct Labour Organizations (DLOs), and could include some caretakers or groundsmen. When a DLO wins a council contract, a governing body will have the right to require that a particular DLO worker be removed from the school.

The LEA as employer

As the previous paragraphs show, governing bodies will exercise considerable powers as the LEA's statutory agents in these employment matters. They involve major decisions about how the school's resources are to be deployed, and matters both sensitive and potentially explosive in selection and industrial relations. Prudent LEAs will probably try to help them in these matters.

LEAs are likely to provide guidelines on many of the matters which fall to governors. These guidelines might usefully suggest, within a range, the number and grade of employees in each main category, selection criteria and procedures, grievance and disciplinary procedures, a range of non-statutory payments for redundancy or premature retirement, arrangements for conciliation, and other matters. All these would be appropriate matters to include in training for heads and other senior staff, and in training for governors.

As a minimum, both heads and governors need to know how the LEA can help them in these employment matters. Chief Education Officers can call on the educational expertise of inspectors and advisers, legal expertise, and the personnel officers' expertise in establishment matters, selection and industrial relations. In addition to this expertise, LEAs also have great experience, arising from their responsibility for a few dozen schools in the smallest LEAs, to a few hundred in the largest.

Also, they have an overall responsibility for ensuring that their institutions can recruit and retain staff. Mutual self-interest suggests that they should publish, and their institutions observe, wise policies and guidelines on the personnel matters which fall within the governors' ambit. Governing bodies and heads will be free to decide whether to adopt the LEA's policies and guidelines, and how far to accept the LEA's advice on specific cases.

Financial matters

Schools and colleges will be able to draw also on their LEA's expertise in financial matters. This is a particularly sensitive aspect of *Local Management of*

Schools because failure here is perhaps the most likely to precipitate a withdrawal of delegated powers.

As in employment matters, governing bodies will have considerable freedom to manage their own finances. Subject to an overriding bar on their incurring deficits or running overdrafts, they will be free to:

- exercise virement;
- use their delegated budget or other funds to buy in additional inservice training, or legal, architectural and other professional services beyond those provided centrally by their LEA;
- redeploy revenue into capital projects;
- make their own arrangements for maintaining their premises;
- retain any savings they make, except for example where an LEA has invested in energy saving;
- raise income and to use the funds they have raised. Any income from lettings or donations would be additional to their formula funding by the LEA;
- carry over unspent balances; and
- enter into commitments for the future.

Schools and colleges must act in accordance with their LEA's rules on such matters as authorizing expenditure, keeping and auditing accounts, and providing the LEA with accounts and records. The LEA's Chief Financial Officer will be responsible for regular audit and will have the right to attend governing body meetings to give advice or present reports.

Governing bodies may value the LEA's help in setting up their financial systems and training staff. The continuing help of skilled auditors should ensure a steady improvement in these systems, and relieve heads and governors of much anxiety. They may also value the LEA's help in appraising the financial consequences of some of the options they will have to consider.

Premises

In their report on *Local Management of Schools*, Coopers and Lybrand suggested the landlord and tenant relationship as an apt analogy for the relationship between an LEA and its schools and colleges.

Like other tenants, governing bodies will be responsible for the day-to-day maintenance of their school premises, and health and safety. They will wish to satisfy themselves that the premises and major equipment are suitable for the National Curriculum. To do this, governing bodies will need up-to-date information on the condition of the premises at the time of delegation and at regular intervals thereafter. They may have to press the LEA to do as Circular 7/88 suggests (para. 73), and provide this information.

As with employment and financial matters, schools and colleges should be able to look to their LEA for information and expertise on maintenance, health and safety, energy conservation, and the design and use of space for education. They should be able to rely on their LEA for a regular programme of capital improvements to keep the school building stock up to date. Indeed, one measure of a school's effectiveness might be its success in persuading its LEA to update its buildings so that they provide for current teaching and learning methods.

Curriculum and assessment

Heads, governors and LEAs all have a statutory duty to ensure that the schools for which they are responsible provide the National Curriculum. But in this the LEA is predominant. By a neat twist, the Education Reform Act giveth, and it taketh away. Schools now have much more responsibility for employment, finance and premises, but much less for the curriculum and assessment. The LEAs have lost control over employment, finance and premises, but have much clearer responsibilities for:

- managing grant-aided programmes, such as those for inservice training, education support projects, TVEI, work-related further education, and education of immigrants [Section 11];[2]
- securing delivery of the National Curriculum and pupil assessment;
- monitoring school performance; and
- advising governors and heads.

The elected members of LEAs have lost much of their quasi-managerial and administrative work to governing bodies, but the Chief Education Officer now has a statutory right (Circular 7/88, paras 158 and 166) to advise governors, and the inspectors have mounting responsibilities for curriculum development, assessment procedures, inservice training and appraisal. The Department of Education and Science has decided to meet part of the cost of at least two more inspectors in each LEA, LEAs are beginning once again to call their advisers 'inspectors', and several have re-established the dormant post of Chief Inspector. It may help schools to work effectively with their LEA if they grasp what it is that LEAs now have to do.

1 *Policy*: they must set out their curriculum policy, a splendid opportunity to fill some of the gaps left by the National Curriculum.
2 *Resources*: they set the local budget, and after consultation, select the formula which determines each school's share of the budget.
3 *Advice*: they advise governors about the LEA's policy, the implications of any school policy for the curriculum, the implications of decisions about how resources are deployed in the school, and the selection of staff.
4 *Assessment*: they monitor every school's performance, and assess the effect of LEA and school decisions about resources; they organize teacher appraisal.

5 *Management*: they manage governor training and services such as Education Social Work, Education Psychology and Careers, in ways which complement their curricular policies.
6 *Development*: they use LEA training grants and education support grants to promote the National Curriculum and LEA curricular policies, and to remedy any perceived weaknesses.

Governing bodies have a statutory right to comment on their LEA's curriculum policies and its plans for local management. They may be more wary about commenting on the other functions described above: advice, assessment, management and development. In these matters the Education Reform Act seems to give the Chief Education Officer (CEO) and inspectors acting for the CEO a degree of independence from the Council which employs them. The whole service might benefit if schools and LEAs were to engage in fruitful dialogue about how the LEA can best perform its newly defined tasks. Schools have legitimate views about how advice and assessment can be most helpfully presented, how the service should be managed and developed. In these, as in other matters, the proper duty of an LEA is to support and negotiate with its schools.

Complaints about the curriculum

One aspect of the Education Reform Act deserves a special note. ERA says little about LEAs, but Clause 23 gives them a key task in relation to the curriculum. Each LEA must establish machinery to hear and deal with complaints made on or after 1 September 1989 about the way in which the LEA or the governing body of any of its schools is exercising its powers in relation to the curriculum.

The panels established to hear complaints will need informed evidence from both the LEA and school in order to decide whether a complaint is justified. If a complaint is upheld the LEA's officers and inspectors must be able to advise governors and the LEA itself precisely what remedial action to take.

In some areas this new system may lead to a spate of enquiries about the National Curriculum and religious education. LEA inspectors may be able to deal with many of these enquiries and prevent them becoming formal complaints.

Even more important, the expert contribution LEA inspectors make to 'the consideration and disposal of any complaint' should be framed so that it is thoroughly helpful to the head and staff. In some cases their evidence will convince the panel that a complaint should be rejected. In the other cases, when a complaint is upheld they will be responsible for helping the governors and the LEA to take whatever remedial action is necessary. Their work as inspectors will enable them to make this supportive contribution when the pressure is greatest.

Support and service from the LEA

Thirty years ago at least one local Education Office was nicknamed 'the Kremlin'. That was before *glasnost* and *perestroika* transformed the Kremlin, and well before competitive tendering and local management led LEAs to restructure their Education Departments. Even without sophisticated information technology systems, the days of large administrative bureaucracies are numbered.

Faced with their own problems, from GCSE and the National Curriculum to teacher shortages and local management, schools may not appreciate the traumas in their local Education Department. As US Secretary of State Foster Dulles said of Britain, the Departments have 'lost an empire, and not yet found a role'.

Their new role seems to lie in providing expert services. The requirement to submit certain services to competitive tender has brought out the difference between contractors, customers and consultants. The contractors provide a service, the customers buy and use that service and, in some circumstances, consultants help the customers to specify what standard of service is required and ensure that that standard is provided.

Until now local authorities have often been both contractor and customer. One obvious example is the school meals service, where the Education Department has been the contractor who provided a service, the customer[3] who paid the bill, and the consultant who specified quality and cost. In future local authorities will have to distinguish clearly between these three functions.

When catering is subject to competitive tender, the Education Department will need a 'consultant' to advise what standards to specify in the tender documents, and how to monitor the service to ensure that the contractor provides a service of the agreed standard. Schools and colleges which choose to run their own catering service may welcome help from the Department's catering consultant.

The Education Department will need to call on similar expertise in other services which are subject to competitive tendering: grounds maintenance, vehicle maintenance and cleaning. Their experts will be available for schools which use their powers under local management to specify the standard of service they require, whether from the LEA's contractor, or their own.

LEAs might usefully provide similar kinds of expertise in other services which are not subject to competitive tendering. As landlord, the LEA will need its own building surveyors, and it will also need some independent expertise on supplies, equipment, and health and safety in order to offer schools and colleges advice on these matters. Some of these services might be provided within the LEA's part of the general schools budget, and others at cost to the users. The idea of schools and colleges buying services from their local authority may sound novel, but it is implicit in local management.

Every local authority department is beginning to grasp this. Unless they provide quality services at a good price, schools and colleges will be free to go elsewhere. The departments have to develop an effective marketing strategy before local management begins to bite.

Grant-maintained schools and LEAs

Local authorities will also be free to offer their services for sale to grant-maintained schools. Grant-maintained schools may well be able to strike a good price with some local authorities for expert advice on a wide range of subjects such as building maintenance, energy conservation, equipment, health and safety, catering, cleaning and transport. Legal, financial, architectural, personnel and other services may be available from the specialist departments, and the Education Department may be able to offer the services of its inspectors, educational psychologists and other experts. LEAs may be happy to provide these services at cost, so that they can go on offering these specialist services to the schools which are still maintained by them. The alternative for LEAs where a relatively high proportion of schools opt for grant-maintained status, taking with them both their formula funding and a proportionate share of the LEA's administrative overheads, will be to start running down their specialist central support staff. As an LEA becomes progressively less able to provide expert advice across the whole curriculum, for example, schools will see fewer benefits in remaining with the LEA, and may be more inclined to consider opting out.

Whether they look to an LEA for those services or not, all grant-maintained schools will have a continuing interest in some LEA decisions. The LEA's funding formulae will determine their own budgets, and the LEA's Careers and Education Social Work Services will work with their pupils. They will have an interest in the LEA's provision of pupil support services, from home to school transport, to clothing and other maintenance allowances, and discretionary awards for higher education.

Some grant-maintained schools may wish to work in partnership with LEA schools or colleges, so as to extend the range of courses that they all can offer. And, for their part, LEAs will have to make arrangements for pupils excluded by grant-maintained schools. These shared concerns point to the need for some regular consultative machinery to enable LEAs and grant-maintained schools in their area to discuss service levels and their delivery.

Conclusion

This chapter has explored some of the many different kinds of links between schools, colleges and their LEAs. As the previous section suggested, even schools which opt out will continue to share some concerns with the LEA and may look to the LEA for certain services.

The variety of the links between schools and their LEA may pose problems for both the schools and the LEA. Their links cover almost every aspect of the institution's life and work. They range from matters where the governors have statutory duties – in determining, for example, what sex education a school shall provide [Education Act (No. 2) 1986, Clause 18] – to matters where the LEA's Chief Education Officer and Chief Financial Officer have statutory rights to advise the governors. They embrace services which schools and colleges buy from the LEA, and programmes and services for which the LEA contracts with outside agencies, such as education support grants, LEA training grants, grants for the education and welfare of immigrants (Local Government Act 1966, Section 11), TVEI, work-related further education, and Department of Employment grants for strengthening the careers service.

For most governing bodies, the question of their relations with the LEA is most likely to arise on some specific issue:

- How should they respond if, for example, the LEA wishes to explore the possibility of community use of school premises, or some collaboration between schools and colleges in post-16 provision?
- How should they respond to the LEA's curricular policies, particularly on cross-curricular issues?
- How should they respond to the LEA inspectors' reports?
- How much weight should they attach to LEA guidelines on staffing levels and the use of their budget?
- How much weight should they attach to LEA guidelines on selection, grievances, discipline or compensation?
- In what circumstances would they be justified in rejecting unequivocal advice from the Chief Education or Financial Officers, or their representatives?
- Should they adopt any non-statutory selection or employment policies the LEA may have?
- What considerations should they have in mind when deciding whether to opt in or out of LEA service contracts?
- Should they ask the LEA to increase the minimum number of pupils they must admit each year if the school happens to have enough accommodation for more pupils?
- What should they do if the LEA seems to be neglecting its responsibilities as landlord?
- How should they respond if the LEA's requests for information seem to be getting out of hand?
- When, if ever, should they threaten to opt out?

These questions give some indication of the range of matters where the governing body and LEA might work in partnership, or in conflict.

In identifying and mobilizing resources for their school or college, governing bodies should acknowledge the LEA as perhaps their greatest potential ally. That understanding might usefully inform their debates on many of these specific issues.

Notes

1 Under the careers service strengthing scheme, announced in 1987, the Department of Employment pays grants to LEAs to strengthen their Careers Service provided the DoE is satisfied with the LEA's 1-year plan and 3-year development programme for their Careers Service.
2 Section 11 Grants in accordance with Section 11 of the Local Government Act 1966. Under this scheme the Home Office pays grants for the education and social welfare of immigrants from the New Commonwealth and Pakistan. The scheme has been used extensively by local authorities and voluntary agencies to support additional posts in teaching, youth work and social work.
3 Until recently, what pupils paid barely met the cost of provisions. LEAs met the much greater costs of accommodation, equipment, fuel and staff.

Bibliography

Education (No. 2) Act 1986. London, HMSO.
Education Reform Act 1988. *Local Management of Schools*. DES Circular 7/88; *Local Management of Further and Higher Education Colleges*, DES Circular 9/88; *Grant Maintained Schools*, DES Circular 10/88. London, HMSO.
Local Government Act 1986. London, HMSO.

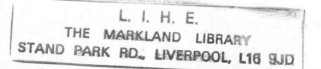

Author index

Subject index